Review

The Trail to Eternity

Kandy has given us a delightful book that weaves together her experiences with horses and the lessons learned in her walk with the Lord.

She writes about the struggles and triumphs in her life with frank honesty. Kandy's passion to share her life with her readers so they can deepen their walk with God is evident. She links Bible verses and commentary to the lessons learned. This book is an enjoyable read. If you want a down-to-earth book that challenges and encourages you in your walk with the Lord - this is the book for you!

— **Dr. Gale Struthers**, Biblical Studies Program Director, *Oak Hills Christian College*

***

The "Trail to eternity" is an epic journey of life experiences, sentimental relationships with nature and horses, and leaps of faith to encourage every reader. This book helps anyone enjoy and respect this short thing called life. Kandy gives a great perspective on how to take steps toward eternity and shares her heart of love for God and people.

—**Bruce A. Rauma,** Senior Pastor Legacy Church.
www.legacychurchmn.com

***

This book was very insightful and inspiring. Filled with thrilling life experiences of hope, faith, and the great outdoors. Full of love and compassion. It is refreshingly honest and incredibly practical. This book is relatable to everyone who seeks truth, honesty, love, and life.

—**Diane Rauma.**

***

I find the author of this book, Kandy Magnan to be an inspiring Believer in our Lord Jesus Christ and I am excited to see where her writings lead her. Kandy has a love for the Lord and a desire to share that love with others. I believe her life experiences and love for nature and especially the horses that she portrays in this devotional book will be a help for those growing in the Lord and those who are not believers.

I know her desire is to see others know the love of the Lord that is only found in accepting Him as Lord and Savior. It is an honor to call Kandy a sister in the Lord.

—Shirley Braaten.

***

Having read Kandy's book, The Trail to eternity, I've come to several conclusions about the purpose of her having created this expression of herself.

She speaks of her life, before knowing God, as a kid, adolescent, young adult, young mother, and as a young wife.

Kandy experiences abuse/severe criticism and ridicule from others. She turns for comfort, to owning a dog, and then, owning a golden horse, and the handling of horses; to deal with, the, then, realities of her life. Kandy's love for them, reciprocated, helped her to overcome; the devastation that had been created in her mind.

She suffered from anxiety and uncertainness when it came to facing confrontations and unfamiliar challenges, an inability to say no to people, and a lack of confidence in herself, and her capabilities.

Through positive excerpts' taken from the Holy Bible and her interpretation of those excerpts, she explains how they worked for her, and helped her to heal, from the inside out.

Her ability to write about these matters and to share her experiences are proof of this healing. This book is invaluable!

I believe Kandy is capable of sharing with others, who like herself, are going through or have gone through similar circumstances; healing them also; with her God-given words.

She supports them by offering alternatives: If people would only hear, and believe in God and his presence among us. They too will be healed!

This book I conclude is a work of "Love."

—Danny & Terry Powers.

***

There's a lot of hard-won wisdom in this book, along with some great storytelling. I think there are lessons there for a lot of people, and what they are is going to depend on where you're at in your life. It is true, as Kandy says, that horses are a lot like people and God seems to work with us much as a good horse person works with the different horses they run across.

—Kim Otterson.

ii

The Trail to Eternity

Come Along for the Ride with Jesus as Our Trail Guide

Kandice K. Magnan

Published by KHARIS PUBLISHING, an imprint of KHARIS MEDIA LLC.

Copyright © 2021 Kandice K. Magnan

ISBN-13: 978-1-63746-023-8
ISBN-10: 1-63746-023-6

Library of Congress Control Number: 2021931079

Unless otherwise noted, Scripture is taken from The Holy Bible, the New International Version (NIV) Used by permission of Biblical, Inc.®
All rights reserved worldwide.

All KHARIS PUBLISHING products are available at special quantity discounts for bulk purchase for sales promotions, premiums, fund-raising, and educational needs. For details, contact:

Kharis Media LLC
Tel: 1-479-599-8657

support@kharispublishing.com
www.kharispublishing.com

Dedication

This book is dedicated in gratitude to God, Jesus and the Holy Spirit. Soli Deo Gloria! Glory to God Alone!

To my husband, Tony, thank you for sharing this life with me. Thank you for the joys that we've shared: the adventures and the lessons that we've learned along this trail of life. Thank you for all your hard work and sacrifices that you've made for us and our herd of "hay burners". Also, thank you for your support and encouragement to me in writing this book.

Special dedication to our children and grandchildren: I am proud of the young men and women that you have grown into! Despite all that you have been through, you have chosen the more difficult path of rising above your circumstances.

Contents

Preface

This is what the Lord says, he who made the earth, the Lord who formed it and established it -the Lord is his name: Call to me and I will answer you and tell you great and unsearchable things you do not know. —Jeremiah 33:2-3

Life is such a strange journey. We are born, raised, go off to school, leave school, and then become adults, before passing into eternity. We experience joys and sorrows, successes and sufferings. We face challenges. Some of them we overcome, some overcome us.

We have people all around us that influence our thinking and our perceptions about the world around us, thus shaping our personalities and our decisions. Some of the people that give us input are wise -and their guidance would be well heeded-, while others are foolish -and we would do well to avoid their advice-.

This book is not a horse training book. As you'll discover in subsequent pages, I don't know much about training horses. Yes, I trained my mare, Goldie, and most recently, our youngest mare, Hope, but by most horse people's standards, she's not well trained. So, please don't approach this book looking to find horse training techniques.

What Goldie and I have developed is more of "partnership" than "horsemanship". The fact that I can ride her came from years of us getting to know one another, growing in love with one another, trying different techniques, learning how one another reacts in different situations and developing trust in one another.

Our riding partnership language is personal and unique to us. Exactly like my faith partnership with God.

My purpose in writing this book is to tell you a little about myself; my life journey and the great and unsearchable things that God has taught me through my horses. I hope that through reading my story, you might gain some encouragement as though you've met a friend who may understand you and what you are going through.

My purpose is not to teach you everything that I've learned, because although I've learned a great deal in my life, my knowledge is still incomplete. Even if I had complete knowledge, I could still only do you justice by providing different options and insights that you might find useful. The words that God has given to me, of which I've included in the following pages, may not be the same words that God speaks to you. I'm presenting what God has spoken to me in my own circumstances. I urge you to seek

God and His will for your life specifically.

My purpose is not to write about all of the trials and suffering that I have experienced. Nor do I want to give Satan more credit than he deserves by disclosing too much of the depths of sin that I've been rescued from. Although those things have been an important catalyst for helping me understand, love, and know God deeper, those are not the things that I want to be the focus of in this book. To be honest, much of the pain that I've endured came from my children's sorrows and suffering, and out of respect for them, I am keeping many of those things private.

My purpose in writing this book is that by using my life lessons as examples, I might be an encouragement to you and point you to the One who loves you fiercely, and has perfect knowledge and wisdom; the only One who has all the answers to all of your questions and problems.

For this reason I kneel before the Father, from whom his whole family in heaven and on earth derives its name. I pray that out of his glorious riches he may strengthen you with power through his Spirit in your inner being, so that Christ may dwell in your hearts through faith. And I pray that you, being rooted and established in love, may have power, together with all the saints, to grasp how wide and long and high and deep is the love of Christ, and to know this love that surpasses knowledge -that you may be filled to the measure of all the fullness of God. - Ephesians 3:14-19

Introduction

YAHWEH, the God of Abraham, Isaac, and Jacob; the God who created everything, knows you and loves you. And he wants you to know him. I'm not talking about *knowing about* Him. I'm talking about really *knowing* Him.

Growing up, I knew about God. I knew about all the things I should and should not do. I even prayed occasionally. However, in my late teenage and young adult years, I began making choices that were leading me down a dangerous destructive path. The hardships and abuses that I suffered from those destructive choices pushed me further and further away from God. I did not take responsibility for my choices, because I saw myself as a victim of my circumstances. Indeed, in many ways, I was a victim, however, seeing myself as a victim and refusing to consider my own contributions to my problems, made me live in a posture of "victimhood". Seeing myself as a victim, I grew angry at God. Fueling this anger was my misunderstanding of God and his character.

My anger began to dissipate eventually, as I refused to acknowledge God at all. I distinctly remember a conversation between coworkers and myself, discussing religion. I boasted that my religion is the religion of "Kandy". In a sense, I was saying that I was my own god. This was when I reached the lowest point of my life.

From a worldly perspective, I was doing ok. I had left my broken marriage, had a great paying job, was making friends, and was" enjoying" life for the first time in decades. Unfortunately, "enjoying" life meant going to the bars and getting drunk every weekend that my children were with their dad. "Enjoying" life meant the thrill of dating again which sometimes included poor judgment on my part and had devastating results.

Looking back, I can see how God put people onto my path as mile markers to guide me on the path to him. He also spoke to me in dreams that were deeply disturbing at the time, and having those dreams become reality months and years later, I now know that God was trying to warn me through them.

I remember one night when the kids were at their dad's, I was sitting in the middle of my living room floor, deeply troubled about the purpose of my life. I remember thinking to myself, "What's wrong with me? I have a great paying job with great benefits, I'm out of my marriage and finally happy. I'm doing pretty darn good, as good as anyone else that I know. Why am I sitting here troubled about my purpose? How many other people sit on their living room floors, struggling with their purpose? Am I going crazy?"

I am convinced that this experience was God's divine intervention. My children, aged 10, 8, 6, and 4 were going to church with a friend while I was at work. Little did I know that they were all praying for me to come to know Jesus.

My salvation experience is so precious to me. I don't remember the date, but I remember clearly the experience. My children talked me into going to church with them. They begged me to come and "learn about God" with them. I really didn't want to go. I had no problem with them going. I felt it was good for them to have that exposure, however, my feeling was, "No thanks. Been there, done that, don't care to do it again." I knew that I was a sinner. I didn't need religious folks to tell me that. But my children insisted, so for their benefit, I agreed to go. Here I was, heading to church with body piercings, tattoos, and a major chip on my shoulder.

I intended to show up, tell the pastor every rotten thing I'd ever done, he'd tell me that I was going to burn in hell for all eternity and then I could leave and never have to come back.

Summer of 2004, holding my children's hands, I walked up the steps to the church. The pastor greeted me and told me that he was so glad to meet me. My thoughts were, "Yeah, right. You tell everybody that." I followed the plan and told him everything I'd determined to say and stood back, with an attitude of "what do you think of me, now?", smugly waiting for his response. He smiled warmly at me and said, "I trust that as you search the Scriptures, God will show you what needs to be changed and he will give you the strength to change it." Huh?" I was dumbfounded and didn't even know how to respond. As I stood there, mentally scratching my head, my children took me by my hands and led me into the church.

We sat down in a pew and I remember watching them in awe. Even at such young ages, they were so well behaved. I had Dylan on one knee, Jenna on the other. Tim was sitting right next to me on one side and Daniel was on the other. They all had their arms wrapped around me, and they were whispering, "I love you, mom" into my ears. They knew all of the songs and sang so beautifully. Tears began streaming down my cheeks. My heart was so full of love that I felt it was going to burst. I didn't even know that this level of love was possible. I didn't want it to ever end. I was hooked and needed to have it every Sunday.

I began learning about how much God loves each one of us, and how Jesus loves each one of us so very much, that he was willing to die for us. It broke my heart knowing the sacrifice that Jesus made because of my sins. I couldn't understand how he could love me when no one seemed to love me.

I did not even love me.

One Sunday, the pastor made an altar call where he asked for anyone who wanted Jesus in their heart, to come forward and receive him through prayer. In my mind, I wanted Jesus, but I didn't feel like I was good enough to receive Jesus. That was how little I understood about grace.

I remember standing there, conflicted about what I should do. I wanted Jesus, but I was afraid of what people would think, seeing me wanting to receive Jesus. I honestly believed that other people were thinking, "Who does she think she is, thinking she is worthy of Jesus?" The next thing I knew, (I'm not kidding) on their own will, my legs started moving, and my feet were taking me up to the front of the church, and that day I gave my life to Jesus. My life has never been the same since.

As God revealed to me the faulty thinking and patterns of behavior that contributed to my suffering, and as he replaced those thinking and behavior patterns with his, I began to feel empowered. I began to realize that the "victim" label that I was wearing, had become a prison that kept me from experiencing a new life. By taking responsibility for my past poor choices, and learning from God how to make better choices, I was able to start making better choices and thus change the direction of my life. As 2 Corinthians 5:17 states, "Therefore, if anyone is in Christ, he is a new creation; the old has gone, the new has come!"

It is truly humbling knowing the distance God will go to help us know him and love him! He knows the very number of hairs on our heads! (Luke 12:7) He knows you and me personally! He knows the family you were born into, the struggles you faced in adolescence, what you have accomplished, and also also the sorrows you have endured and your future. He knows the questions that you have like, *Why?" What do I do next?" How do I handle this?" Does anyone really care about me?"* I don't know you, but I'm quite certain that you've had your share of sorrows and suffering. Perhaps at this very moment you're struggling and wondering if God exists, does he even see you? Does he even care?

Believe it or not, he even wants to hear about your anger and frustration. In Psalms 13, 35, 80, and 90 king David cried out to God in anguish, *How long, O, Lord?* It may surprise you, but God called David a man after his own heart! God knows that we are humans with limited knowledge and ability to understand, especially those things that are supernatural. However, God looks at our hearts. He knows that we struggle with our emotions and he wants us to come to him with them, especially our anger. God is big enough; he can handle your anger. The key is going to him in honesty, with a heart that wants healing. A heart that doesn't want to be angry. A heart that truly wants to understand, grow and change. James 4:7-8 tells us, "Submit yourselves, then, to God. Resist the devil and he will flee from you. Draw near to God and he will draw near to you. Wash your hands you sinners, and purify your hearts, you double-minded." So, how do we get to know God? We absolutely need to be reading the Bible.

2 Timothy 3:16-17 tells us that "All Scripture is God-breathed and is useful for teaching, rebuking, correcting and training in righteousness, so that the servant of God may be thoroughly equipped for every good work." If you are not a believer of Jesus and the Bible doesn't make sense to you, it may be because it was written to guide servants of God -believers of Christ-. The Scriptures were given to teach believers how to love God and love others by learning to live in righteousness.

Some things within the Bible are hard to understand. A wonderful Bible study tool is https://www.biblehub.com. This website has the many different translations of the Bible to help you study the Scriptures across the different translations. It has tools for you to look up specific words in the original Hebrew and Greek languages and learn their meanings. You can look up how often some words occur throughout the Bible and in what contexts. It also has commentaries written by several different Bible scholars that you can read to get insight into what the text meant to the original hearers and how it may apply to you today. A couple of other great online Bible study websites are https://www.biblegateway.com and https://www.blueletterbible.org. I encourage you to explore these websites and see what they have to offer you. There are Bible study books that you can buy online at https://www.christianbook.com. Another great resource is https://koinoniainstitute.org/ where you can learn valuable tools for gaining scholarly Biblical study. Other helpful tools are books on ancient Jewish history and traditions. These help you to understand the Jewish culture so you'll have an easier time understanding what the Scriptures meant to the original hearers. You can purchase commentaries on the Bible. These commentaries can either be on the entire Bible or for a particular book in the Bible. There are so many resources available for you to go as deep as you'd like to in knowing God.

Before taking the Bible to study, ask God to help clear your mind so that you can focus on the Scriptures. Also, ask the Holy Spirit to point out to you specific Scriptures that are important for you personally, and. help you understand how it applies to you. When studying the Bible look for repetitive words, sentences and themes. Repetition indicates importance. Additionally, look for words such as "therefore", "and", "but", etc. These add emphasis to the text and indicate important ideas that you should pay attention to. When studying a specific Scripture, study the Scriptures immediately preceding and following to get the context of the Scripture you are studying. Look for contrasts and/or comparisons.

These are just beginning tools to help you get started. The beauty of the Bible is that God designed it so that it is simple enough for a child to understand, yet there are gold mines of amazing insights for those who desire to dig deeper.

The Bible is His user's manual about Him and how He relates to His creation. It is also His user's manual for us on how we are to relate to Him and His creation, specifically other people.

A cautionary statement: His manual shouldn't be used to condemn people, including ourselves. Condemnation is God's job and He provided Jesus so that anyone who might believe in him (Jesus) would not be condemned but be saved for eternity (John 3:16-18) If you have given your life to Jesus, you are free from condemnation (Romans 8:1).

If you haven't given your life to Jesus, I would strongly urge you to consider doing so. We have been created to be eternal beings, meaning that despite physical death, we still have an eternal destiny. Those who have accepted Jesus will live eternally with him, likewise, those who've rejected him will live eternally apart from him, in a place known as hell.

Many people stumble at this point, asking questions such as, "If God is such a loving God, why would he send people to hell just because they don't accept Jesus?" Their understanding of God is incomplete. God is a holy God. Because of his holiness, he cannot look upon sin. God created Adam and Eve. They were perfect in every way, and God loved and hung out with them in the garden of Eden every day. It was wonderful until the devil came along. At one time, he was one of God's most beautiful angels, but because of his pride and desire to become equal to God, he was cast out of heaven and sent to earth (See Isaiah 14:12-15 and Ezekiel 28:12-19). He's jealous because he knows that humanity is God's dearest and beloved creation; so beloved to God that God Himself destined us to reign with him. Satan knows God's standards better than any human. He also knows humans better than we know ourselves and he knew what he needed to do to make Adam and Eve suffer and die. So, he confused and cast doubt into Eve regarding God's words and God's goodness. Then he tempted her into eating the forbidden fruit. Eve then convinced Adam into eating the fruit. God, being a just God who can't tolerate sin had to punish them for their sin. He just had to. He wouldn't be just if he didn't punish sin. Even though he loved Adam and Eve so very much, because he is just in addition to love, he had to punish them for their disobedience; so, God punished both Adam and Eve together with the serpent.

Now, since sin came through Adam and Eve, every human being born from them is born with sin in them. God still loves humans and desires a close personal relationship with them, but how does God reconcile the apparent conflict between his love and his justice? He developed a system for cleansing them and making them holy to enjoy fellowship with him. That system was a complicated set of rules and regulations that included animal sacrifice -the spilling of blood -to pay the penalty for breaking all the rules.

Some people might be offended by this, thinking that it's terrible for an animal to lose its life through sacrifice. Yes, they would be right. God used a method that would make a tremendous impression on each person.

In the garden of Eden, when Adam and Eve sinned, their eyes were opened and they saw that they were naked. So, then they used fig leaves to cover themselves. Knowing that fig leaves were not adequate covering for them, God sacrificed an animal-one of the animals that Adam himself, had named, and used the skins for clothing for them. The animal served as a sacrifice for covering of physical protection and spiritual atoning. It cost the animal everything to provide what Adam and Eve needed. This instance is the first example of humans trying to cover themselves -trying to make their own way of covering their sins, but proving that their efforts come up short, and God himself, providing a better way. Every animal onward that was to be offered as a sacrifice, was to be the owner's personal best. It had to really cost the owner. He/she couldn't offer a lame one, or a blind one, or one that had blemishes or defects. It couldn't be one that no one else wanted. It had to be his best. Perhaps this animal may have even been a family pet, likely living in the house with them.

Before the building of the tabernacle and temple, the people raised their animals for sacrifices by themselves, and it was their responsibility to kill the animal and offer it as a sacrifice. I believe that God wanted them to experience the ugliness of taking an innocent animal and killing it, showing them in living color, that this is what it took to cleanse them of their own sins; to impress upon the people, that sin is costly. I also believe that God was setting the stage all those thousands of years ago, for humanity to understand the most costly sacrifice of all which is Jesus Christ. Jesus ushered in the new covenant between God and humanity.

Romans 3:20 states that the purpose of the law (the 10 commandments) was to make people aware of what God's requirements are and how impossible it is for people to wholly keep the law in their own abilities. It is basically a way for us to see the contrast between a holy God and sinful humans.

Jesus was conceived of the Spirit, and born of a virgin, Mary. Basically, he's God in flesh. Therefore, since he was conceived by the Spirit and not through the physical union of a human man and a human woman, he was conceived with no natural sin, and with no sin nature, he grew up without sin. He is fully human and fully God, making him the only sinless human who ever lived. He was God's own perfect sacrifice, and he was sacrificed for our sins. Jesus became sin, so that by sacrificing his life, the penalties for all sin past, present and future, committed by all humans would be paid in full. I found this hard to grasp at first. Jesus actually became sin so that all of God's holy wrath for sin was poured out onto Jesus. 2 Corinthians 5:21 states that, "God made him (Jesus) who had no sin to be sin for us so that in him we might become the righteousness of God."

Thus, Jesus was sent to be the covering of holiness that we need and the sacrifice that God requires for the atonement of sin. Isn't that great news? No more sacrificing of different animals to atone for our many different sins throughout our lives. No more frantic worrying if our "good" deeds out-weigh our "bad" deeds and if it's enough to get us into heaven! Jesus' once and for all sacrifice is sufficient to atone all of the sins we've ever committed and any of our future sins that we will commit!

The old order of law was necessary for that time frame. Upon Jesus' death, that order was abolished and the new order of grace came into effect. Because of Jesus' sacrifice, if we accept his sacrifice for our sins, we are made right with God and granted direct access to him! Under the old law, only the chosen high priest had access to God on behalf of the people. And the high priest had to go through strict regulations before he could come before God.

When we accept Jesus' sacrifice as atonement for our sins, his righteousness is applied to us and we are granted direct access to God -as we are-. As Romans 3:22 states, "This righteousness (the righteousness of God) is given through faith in Jesus Christ to all who believe."

Accepting Jesus' sacrifice is simply acknowledging the reality of the ugliness of our sin, and our inability to make ourselves holy on our own, believing that Jesus was the perfect sacrifice for our sins, and being willing to follow his lead in our lives. When Jesus died on the cross, one of the last things he said was, "Tetelestai" meaning, "It is finished" and/or "Paid in full". So, by accepting Jesus' sacrifice for your sins, you are assured that your sin debt, by Jesus' sacrifice, is paid in full.

God, by providing Jesus, and raising Jesus from the dead, made the way for us to be holy so that we can enjoy an everlasting relationship with him. Therefore, anyone who refuses Jesus' sacrifice is themselves, choosing to spend eternity apart from him. The blame cannot be placed on God. He has done everything to make possible the way for every human to have eternal life with him. Respecting the free will of each person, he allows each person to choose for him/herself, where they want to spend eternity. So, anyone spending eternity apart from Jesus has done so of their own free will.

If there is any confusion as to the depth of the love of God, a person only needs to study Jesus and how he loved people. Jesus himself tells us that by knowing him, we know the Father (John 14).

Once we have accepted Jesus' sacrifice for our sins, God sends the Holy Spirit to live in us and teach us. Jesus himself stated this in John 16:13; "But when he; the Spirit of truth comes, he will guide you into all truth." As we read God's Word, the Holy Spirit helps us understand how to apply God's Word to our own lives. Even though the debt of sin has been canceled, as human beings, living in a sin-filled world, we are still susceptible to falling into temptation.

The Holy Spirit helps us recognize when we're being tempted and he helps us run away from that temptation. He helps break the chains of habit and addictions that keep us enslaved to sins. Paul writes to us in Romans 8:13, "For if you live according to the flesh, you will die; but if by the Spirit you put to death the misdeeds of the body, you will live." Again, Paul writes in 1 Corinthians 10:13, "No temptation has overtaken you except what is common to mankind. And God is faithful; he will not let you be tempted beyond what you can bear. But when you are tempted, he will also provide a way out so that you can endure it." When we are tempted. Not if we are tempted.

Being tempted is part of life. Even Jesus was tempted. Luke writes in Luke 4:1-2, "Jesus, full of the Holy Spirit, left the Jordan and was led by the Spirit into the wilderness, where for forty days he was tempted by the devil." Did you catch that? Jesus--full of the Holy Spirit--was led BY the Spirit -into the wilderness TO BE tempted by the devil. James explains to us the purpose of the testing in James 1:2-3. "Consider it pure joy, my brothers and sisters, whenever you face trials of many kinds, because you know that the testing of your faith produces perseverance." Peter also explains this in 1 Peter 1:6-8. "These (trials and suffering) have come so that the proven genuineness of your faith -of greater worth than gold, which perishes even though refined by fire- may result in praise, glory and honor when Jesus Christ is revealed."

Jesus (God in the flesh) was showing us by example that there is a necessary purpose in temptations, trials and sufferings; the strengthening and proving of our faith. Additionally, Jesus gave us an example of how to withstand temptation. When you read about Jesus' temptation, we see that the devil tempted Jesus in three ways. The first instance was, because of fasting for 40 days and nights, Jesus was hungry, so the devil tells him, "If you are the Son of God, tell this stone to become bread." I believe that in addition to appealing to Jesus' human physical need (food) he's also cynically calling into question, the truth of Jesus' deity to incite Jesus to use his powers to satisfy his needs. He did the same thing with Eve in the garden. Genesis 3:6," Eve saw that the fruit was good for food, pleasing to the eye, and also desirable for gaining wisdom."

Jesus withstood the temptation by quoting Scripture. Then the devil led Jesus to a high place and showed him all the kingdoms of the world and tempted him by saying, "I will give you all their authority and splendor, for it has been given to me, and I can give it to anyone I want to. So, if you worship me, it will all be yours." Satan already knew that God promised that Jesus would become King of all the kingdoms of the world. What he's offering Jesus here is a way out of the cross. He was tempting Jesus to take a shorter, easier way to what God had already promised. Similarly, he tempted Eve by saying, "You will not surely die, For when God knows that when you eat of it your eyes will be opened, and you will be like God, knowing good and evil" (Genesis 3:4-5). Again, Jesus withstands the temptation by quoting Scripture. Lastly, the devil led Jesus to Jerusalem and had him stand on the highest point of the temple and said, "If you are the Son of God, throw yourself down from here, for it is written, 'He will command his angels concerning you, to guard you carefully; they will lift you with their hands so that you will not strike your foot against a stone." Again, he is calling into question God's faithfulness as well as Jesus' deity, I would say it's like taunting someone saying, "I dare you..." to prove themselves. I believe that he's also attempting to cause Jesus to prove that God really does care about him and will rescue him. Additionally, this is evidence of Satan knowing the Scriptures, himself, and trying to use them for his own purposes (of tempting). That is another tactic of the devil. He takes what God created as good and twists it for evil use. Once again, Jesus quoted Scriptures and the devil left him.

Satan's tactics remain the same when it comes to us. Using our weaknesses, he tempts us to satisfy our physical, emotional, or spiritual needs in whatever way necessary. He tempts us with our eyes -causing us to lust and envy, tempting us to get what we want; even convincing us that we "deserve" it. He also tempts us into believing that we can be "like" God; in effect, we can be our own gods. If God has promised us something, Satan tempts us with doubt that God can/will deliver on his promises, that opens up the temptation to make it happen ourselves. The danger is that Satan seeks to destroy, kill and devour us. He tempts us into sinning, then torments us with accusations for that sinning. See Zechariah 3:1-2 and Revelation 12:10.

Hebrews 2:18 explains to us that, "Because he (Jesus), himself suffered when he was tempted, he can help those who are being tempted." Additionally, in Hebrews 4:15 we are told of Jesus, "For we do not have a high priest who is unable to sympathize with our weaknesses, but we have one who has been tempted in every way, just as we are -yet was without sin-." God came to earth in the form of a human baby who was named Jesus, so that as a fellow human, he could relate to our human experience, and show us how to overcome by the power of the Spirit.

Even with the Spirit's help, we are still imperfect, and we don't always heed the Spirit's instruction. Praise God that we are covered under his grace. I've heard 1 John 1:9 called the Christian's bar of soap. It states, "If we confess our sins, God is faithful and just to forgive us our sins and purify us from all unrighteousness." Being a personal God, he knows that each of us has different life experiences and backgrounds, making learning about him different and unique even from members of our own families. That's why it is so important to make him the ultimate authority over our lives. Again, it is good to seek wisdom from Godly people, but ultimately our decisions need to be made from the Word of God.

How do horses fit into all of this? God knows that as human beings, some of us learn better with visual examples or living parables. Romans 1:20 tells us, "For since the creation of the world God's invisible qualities -his eternal power and divine nature- have been clearly seen, being understood from what has been made, so that people are without excuse." God uses everything to teach us about himself. That is how much he loves us. He uses every means possible, knowing that each of us learns differently than others.

I am an "outdoor" person. I grow in knowing God and connecting with him more deeply when I'm in nature, but God has also used other people, the different relationships that I have and my life circumstances to help me understand him better. He wants us to know him and to continue on a journey of knowing him deeper.

My prayer for you is that through this book, you will embark on this wild, lifelong journey; fully committed to knowing God and growing in your relationship with him, through studying his Word. So, what do you say, friend? Are you ready to saddle up and join me on the trail for the ride of your life?

Abba Father, I pray for the very person reading this book. That you would touch their heart and meet them right where they're at. I pray, Father, that you would reveal to them just how deep and wide and vast is your love for them. I pray that you would draw their hearts into a deeper love and understanding of you. I pray that they would know you and that they would hear your voice leading them in the paths in which they should go. Father give them wisdom and discernment in all of their relationships, human and animal. Teach them the great and unsearchable truths that you have for them. Give them the courage and peace to follow you and you alone. Thank you, Jesus, for all that you have done and all that you are going to do. We love you. In your name, we pray. Amen.

Chapter 1

In the Beginning...

The Lord God said, "It is not good for the man to be alone. I will make a helper suitable for him. Now the Lord God had formed out of the ground all the beasts of the field and all the birds of the air. He brought them to the man to see what he would name them; and whatever the man called each living creature, that was its name. So the man gave names to all the livestock, the birds of the air, and all the beasts of the field. —Genesis 2:18-20

I don't about know you, but perhaps you're a lot like me. I've always related better to animals than to other humans. For as long as I can remember, I've struggled with feeling "socially awkward". I have difficulty knowing what to say and how to say it. Small talk feels clunky and awkward for me. Get me on a topic that I'm passionate about and I'll talk your ears off for hours. Unfortunately, that leads to its own social problems. It is not polite to dominate conversations, especially if the topic is boring to your listeners. I have struggled with being a bit neurotic about my social interactions. There are times -even currently- when I go home and worry myself sick, playing conversations over and over again in my head, wondering whether I had said something that sounded rude, insensitive, egocentric, etc.

I believe that "shyness" is a personality trait that I was born with, however, in the argument of nature versus nurture, I am convinced that my social anxiety is a trauma response from childhood, adolescence, and young adulthood. My first experience with stomach ulcers was when I was in third grade. I had a teacher who was very harsh and would humiliate me and a few other students in front of the class. As I got older, I became the object of tremendous bullying and public humiliation within the halls of our high school, simply because I was considered by some of my peers as "ugly" and "inferior". I was taught by those peers that because they believed that I had no value and was "beneath" them, that I should avoid making eye contact and avoid talking to those "superior" to me; otherwise, I was penalized with more public humiliation and/or physical abuse. So, for much of my adolescence, I went out of my way to try to make myself as invisible and insignificant as possible. If I wasn't noticed, then my chances of surviving the day were greater.

Carrying that label of "no value" into my young adulthood, you can imagine how extremely flattered I was when any guy showed me attention. It is strange how critical having a sense of your own value is in how you perceive who you are as a person, and how you perceive the world around you and your place in it.

As an 18-year-old, I was grateful that any man thought I had some value, but without sensing my own value, and no consideration of how I ought to be treated, I allowed myself to enter a severely abusive and even life-threatening relationship. Being beaten and choked nearly to unconsciousness was a frequent experience for me at that time in my life. Some of the trauma that I've survived includes frequent death threats including having a knife waved in my face and being threatened to be cut into pieces so small that no one would recognize my body. By God's unmerited grace, I was able to miraculously get out of this relationship. Not too long after, however, I jumped into another unhealthy relationship, which led to my first marriage and then divorce. This was my life. I've stared down the barrel of a gun pointed at my forehead. I've looked death straight in the face so many times, that I no longer feared death; In fact, I longed for it. This part of my story is long and complicated; one that I don't want to spend too much time on because I don't want to make it the focus of this book.

My inability to recognize my worth created a failure on my part, to establish and defend boundaries even with strangers, which put me in unsafe situations. You can see the perpetual cycle, right? All of these incidences fueled a struggle with self-acceptance.

It wasn't until I was in my mid-twenties, after my divorce and after giving my life to Jesus, that I first began to recognize and appreciate my worth. I'll never forget the conversation that the pastor and I had regarding dating. The pastor said to me, "You have a responsibility to be very picky about who you date."

I remember being dumbfounded when I asked him, "You mean, I have a right to be picky?"

He replied," You not only have a right, you have a responsibility."

Up to that point, I had the mindset that I needed to be thankful for any guy who showed interest in me. Isn't it strange how much influence the way we speak to and treat others shapes how they interpret who they are and how they fit in the world? Proverbs 12:18 states, "The words of the reckless pierce like swords, but the tongue of the wise brings healing."

As our Creator, God knows each of us personally and intimately. He knows the struggles that we will go through and he uses whatever means are necessary to help us heal, learn and grow. I believe that God created animals specifically to help us, even if it is just for certain seasons in our lives. Have you had the opportunity to experience the love of an animal? I have been loved by animals, and I've learned to love because of animals. I've also learned about my relationship with God and other people through my relationships with my animals.

I was 9 years old when my mom and dad got our first horse. Mom married my stepdad (whom I call 'dad') and we moved from our little apartment in southern MN to our new home in north-central MN. It was dad's dream to have his own dairy farm. We started with a couple of steers named Duke and Nate, a lone dairy cow named Sally, and a horse named Brandy. Dad continued to live and work in southern MN during the week, coming up on weekends, while my mother, my younger sister, and I managed the "farm" up north. Later, dad would quit his machinist job to do farming full time, and our family would grow by 3 more siblings.

Brandy was an untouched mare that came off of dad's brother's farm. I don't remember exactly how old she was when we got her, but. I think she was between a year and two years old. I remember standing back at the trailer when they pulled up by the barn to unload her. I was excited and in awe of her. She was the most beautiful animal I'd ever seen. I remember thinking that she looked like sunshine. I later learned that she was a chestnut. I didn't know any of that at that age. I just knew she was beautiful. Her mane, tail and coat glistened brightly, reflecting the sun at different angles.

She was raising a ruckus in the trailer, terrifying me that an animal so beautiful could also be so powerful. They opened the trailer gate and she bolted out, straight through our barbed wire fence, gashing open her knee. Mom and dad had built a stall for her and were able to coax her into the barn. They called the vet and for the next several months, mom doctored her every day.

Mom also had a love of horses and used to ride at a local horse barn in southern MN. Dad had grown up on a dairy farm (on the land that we were now living on) and they had horses. So, mom and dad set out on working on training Brandy. I don't remember much of the time that mom and dad spent working with Brandy. All I know is that it must have taken a lot of time and love to get Brandy from being wild and scared, to curious, friendly, and willing to be ridden. Mom and dad were both animal lovers and taught us the importance of responsibility in taking care of one's animals. Once we got truly into dairy farming, dad's mantra was "we don't eat until after the cows have eaten". Mom and dad always had the utmost respect for our animals. I remember hearing dad tell mom about the excessive punishment that some people used when training their horses, and how much it angered and disgusted him. Even as a 10 or 11-year-old hearing these conversations began shaping my attitudes about animal husbandry.

I remember standing around watching Brandy, and begging my folks, "when can I ride her?" Finally, dad put me up on top of her with just a halter and a lead rope. He held the lead rope and lead me around on her back as mom walked beside me. I loved the feeling of Brandy's mane in my fingers and the softness of her fur.

I "rode" like this for what seemed like eternity to me. Every day, mom and dad would let me "ride" Brandy. Then dad graduated us to using a bridle. He had the halter and lead rope under the bridle so that he could walk along. Mom walked beside us with her hand near my knee. I will never forget the day that I graduated to riding without assistance. I was riding with mom and dad beside me, and then they let me try to go off on my own. The next thing I knew, Brandy was taking off one way, and I was licking dirt on the ground. Mom and dad came running and once they saw that I was okay, dad said, "Ya gotta get back on." So, this was how I learned to ride.

I loved Brandy. I loved the feeling of being on her back and I was determined to ride. And so, that is how it was. Every day I'd get on, fall off, then get back on. Eventually, Brandy and I were racing around our many acres of pasture.

I loved her; man, I loved her. I remember coming home the day after a brutal day of school, changing into chore clothes and going straight out to talk to Brandy. She was my best friend. My confidant. My favorite times were going out to the pasture, seeing her laying out in the sun. I'd sit on the ground with her, snuggled in the hollow between her shoulder and her belly, sharing my apple with her, as I'd cry to her about the mean kids at school. Have you ever experienced the love and comfort of an animal during your deep sorrows? Animals are such a blessing. Without saying a word, they can help us feel understood and accepted--just as we are.

I remember times when Brandy and I would race across the pasture, going down cattle trails, weaving between the trees and dodging low hanging branches. On Brandy's back, I felt like I wasn't me. Or maybe it was the 'me' that I wanted to be but hadn't yet discovered. I don't know.

Brandy loved me too. I know this because of how she willingly went along with all of my shenanigans. But she retained her own personality and mind. She always found opportunities to humble me and remind me that she has the right to choose to partner with me or not. There were times when I remember charging across the pasture, intending to jump over a fallen tree, and Brandy would come to a dead stop, dropping her head between her legs, and I would find myself lying on my back looking up at her. Eventually, I got to the point where I could at least hang on with both my arms and legs wrapped around her neck, looking up at her like a sloth hanging from a tree. Other times, she would follow the fence so closely, that I'd have to drape my right leg over her back and ride "side saddle" or risk scratching my legs with the barbed wire. Another trick that she would play was walking right next to the barn so that I'd have to duck my head to avoid hitting it on the rafters.

According to today's standards, she was not very well trained. But looking back on it, I guess that's what made our relationship so special. Brandy loved me and it's evidenced by her tolerance of me. She really didn't have to co-operate. We were never abusive to Brandy. and never "beat her into submission. Mom and dad taught me to allow her to be who she was: a horse. It was for me to figure out how I was going to make this partnership work. I think Brandy knew that no matter how many times she threw me off, I was going to get back on. And so eventually, she just quit throwing me off. I think what made us get along so well was our mutual love, respect and acceptance of each other.

After I moved away from home, Brandy became my sister's best friend. A few years later, mom and dad began selling out of the dairy business. Brandy was sold to the auctioneer who bought a bunch of our cattle. I reached out to him many years later to ask him about Brandy. He said that he'd been "hoping to hear from the girl who trained Brandy", so that he could, "thank her." He told me that she had stayed with him and his family until she passed away a couple of years prior, well into her 30's. She was his wife's and grandchildren's best friend. He told me that she was the best darn horse he'd ever owned and that he doubted that he'd ever find another like her. I smiled with tears in my eyes and told him that he was probably right, but that now, at 38 years old, I had a mare of my own, who shares a relationship with me similar to the relationship that Brandy and I had. She is a Golden Palomino and her name is Goldie, and I think she looks just like sunshine.

I couldn't have been prepared for what God had planned for my future. In giving me Brandy, he was setting the stage for a lifetime of learning about him, others and myself, through my love of horses.

Sit deep in the saddle and give a squeeze because we're gonna race along this stretch of the trail!

Chapter 2

Powers Golden Nugget

Every good and perfect gift is from above, coming down from the Father of the heavenly lights, who does not change like shifting shadows. —James 1:17

It was a morning in April 2005, and I was at work when I got a phone call from Danny. "Fancy's having her baby!" Danny said on the other end of the line. Danny and his wife, Terry had just gotten into the horse breeding business. They had two mares that were in foal at the time. Fancy, a blue roan mare, and Ginger, a red roan mare. were both bred to a golden buckskin stud named Tango and due to foal any day now.

Danny and I worked together at a state-operated group home for adults with disabilities and had become good friends. Danny is an eclectic kinda guy. He was a former truck driver, construction worker, cowboy kinda guy with a subtle southern drawl. Stereotypically a tough guy, but having a soft spot that betrayed his teddy bear heart. I spent a lot of time visiting him and his wife on their farm, and loved spending time with their horses. They encouraged me to indulge my horse addictions at their home. I told them of my childhood horse Brandy, and how my parents and I trained her. I spent so much time there that we became like family. I was happy and excited for them to welcome this new little addition to their family.

"Oh, how exciting for you!" I exclaimed to Danny over the phone.

"Yup, we've been keeping an eye on her for the last few hours." Danny paused as he heard Terry hollar in the background. "Gotta go, kid! Gotta get back to Fancy."

Danny hung up the phone and I got back to work. It wasn't too long after, the phone rang and once again, it was Danny. "Fancy had her baby!" Danny reported to me.

"Congratulations!" I was practically jumping up and down, myself.

"It's a little white filly." Danny described to me. "Kid, you might wanna come out here right after work. It looks like she's gonna be an ugly little palomino."

Oh, that was not fair. I told Danny and Terry several months ago about my favorite childhood toy that my parents got me for Christmas one year. It was

6

a Barbie doll palomino filly named Dixie. She was the most beautiful color of horse I'd ever seen. For the record, I never saw a real live palomino before, but right then and there, I knew in my heart that I wanted my very own real palomino colored horse when I got older.

After work, I drove out to Danny and Terry's place and there in the round pen with Fancy was this adorably gangly little bundle of fluff! Even after only a few hours of life, she was prancing around her mama. Granted, it wasn't very graceful, but being an ungraceful person myself, I admired her determination. Standing on the outside of the round pen, I peered between the bars.

"She's so adorable!" I gushed. Her coat reminded me of a creamy apricot color. "So, what are you thinking? You think she'll really be palomino, or do you think she'll be white?"

"It's hard to say," Danny replied, "but by the looks of those eyelashes, I'm guessing she'll turn out to be a palomino."

Looking closely at her eyelashes, I could see a hint of gold. Her baby-fine mane also appeared to have a gold hint in it, as did her stubby little tail. I extended my arm through the bars of the round pen panel, reaching my hand out to hopefully coax her to come near enough for me to pet her.

"Ya wanna go in and pet her?" Danny asked me. "Fancy's had time to bond with her, and she's let us in there to mess with the baby already."

My eyes lit up and my heart skipped a beat. "Yes, please!" I told Danny.

He opened the gate and I very quietly entered the round pen. That little filly was born with such an inquisitive personality that she walked right up to me almost immediately! Reaching out my hand, I stroked her soft velvety muzzle, then slowly began working my way up the side of her face to her mane. I stroked her mane and combed my fingers through it.

"Whatever you do on one side, ya gotta do on the other side" Danny said to me from outside the round pen. I slowly moved around to the other side and did the same. "Rub her all over. She's gotta be comfortable with being touched everywhere."

Her calm demeanor captivated me. It was a stark contrast to everything I was feeling inside of myself. Inside, I was a raging tornado of depression and anxiety. Her calmness and curiosity drew something in my spirit towards her like a magnet. Squatting down in front of her, I looked into her eyes. Ah, the innocence and trust in those eyes. Her eyes revealed a blank slate, or an unwritten book, ready to be filled with pages of adventure and...perhaps love?

"Now take a breath and breathe into her nostrils." Danny's voice broke me from my gaze. Taking a breath, I cupped my hands around her muzzle and blew gently into both of her nostrils. "All this is called imprinting" Danny informed me. "We want her to be exposed to people as soon as possible and for all of her early experiences to be positive. We want her to trust people. That'll make training easier." Fancy began to nicker and the filly left me to prance over to her mama. "Well, kid. What do ya think of her?" Danny asked me as he opened the gate, letting me out of the round pen.

"Oh, she's absolutely perfect!" I replied, grinning from ear to ear.

"Well, do you want her?"

"What?" I didn't know whether to laugh or cry. "Danny, there's no way that I could buy a horse." I stated to him. Here I was, a divorced mother of four young children. I was renting a farmhouse, which fortunately was big enough for all of us and our dog Dozie, but there was no logical way that I could own a horse!

"Well, you could keep her here and pay us board. And you'd be responsible for paying for all of her hay, grain, vaccinations, and all farrier and vet bills." Danny offered.

"Danny, I still don't know…" I started to explain.

"Kid, I know how much you've always wanted a palomino and we're willing to help you out. So, do you want her or not?" Danny was getting impatient at this point.

"Yes! Absolutely, yes!" I took a deep breath and swallowed hard, unbelieving what I had just committed to.

"Good." Danny said with a twinkle in his eye. "Now we gotta get to naming her." Looking back at how the sun shone through her mane, I proudly piped out, "How about Sunshine? My dad always used to call me Sunshine, and it's like she's my sunshine in the darkness."

No matter how hard Danny tried, he couldn't hide the look of disapproval on his face. "Oh, brother. I guess if that's what ya want? But she's gotta have three names for registration."

"Oh, she doesn't need to be registered" I replied.

"Kid, I know that you'll love her regardless of whether she's registered or not, but registration does increase the value of a horse in today's market."

"It doesn't increase her value in my market. No piece of paper is gonna make me love her any more or any less than I already do." I argued.

"Ok, then look at it this way." Danny continued to explain. "Registering a horse is like having a title to a car. It makes you the owner."

This piqued my attention. This would make the little filly legally mine. I wouldn't have to worry about anyone having the right to take her from me. "Okay. I'm game."

"So, to start with, what do you think about using our last name in her registered name?" Danny suggested. I liked that idea. What more fitting way to offer tribute to someone who was giving me my childhood dream? Danny stood looking at her from outside the round pen. "Do you see any markings on her, kid?"

The question startled me. "I guess I didn't even look," I replied. We walked around the perimeter of the round pen to be able to look over every inch of her. "The only thing I see is a tiny white splotch on her forehead," I informed Danny.

"Yeah, me too. Tiny is right. Not even really enough to be considered a star." Danny replied. "Kinda reminds me of a nugget" he went on to say. "Kid, what do you think of the name 'Powers Golden Nugget'?"

"Ooo, I like that. Makes her sound really valuable, like she's my Golden Nugget!" I answered. "Yeah, I like that! Powers Golden Nugget it is, and we'll call her 'Goldie' for short!" I chimed.

It would be over a decade later that I would discover another meaning to Goldie's name. A literal Golden Nugget is a piece of gold produced through mining and extraction, but the phrase "golden nugget" is also used when determining "the most important lesson". Using both definitions together, would imply mining and extracting the most important, useful, and valuable lesson. Little did I know that throughout my life, God would use this metaphor through my Goldie, to help me mine and extract the most important, useful and valuable lessons about Him.

"Take Delight in the Lord, and he will give you the desires of your heart." Psalm 37:4. God is not a genie in a lamp, here to grant our every wish. He's not a vending machine, ready to dispense our every need and want. However, God is a Father who delights in giving gifts to his children. Jesus, himself, said in Matthew 7:11 and Luke 11:13 "If you, then, though you are evil, know how to give good gifts to your children, how much more will your Father in heaven give good gifts to those who ask him!" Our Father "loves us so much that he gave us his only begotten son, that whoever believes in him shall not perish but have everlasting life." John 3:16. Additionally, I believe that because he loves us so much, he cares about all the little details in our lives, giving us gifts that are meaningful to us, personally.

I had a friend who was experiencing great sorrow. Her husband had left her and her children and she had to move to a new home. She recalled to me that during her moments of crying out to God, she cried, "Lord, wherever you take me. Would you please make sure it has lilacs? You know how I love lilacs." Sure enough, the place that he brought her to, had hedges and hedges of lilacs. She told me that she felt in her spirit that this was a symbol of the deep, personal, intimate relationship between only her and God.

Years earlier, I had a couple of similar experiences. I cannot talk about the miracles in my life without talking about my girl, Dozie. I was separated from my then-husband and a single mother of 4. I was lonely and really wanted a dog. I was enamored with Rottweilers. I called every pet store in the phone book looking for Rottweiler puppies. The very last pet store that I contacted said that she had no puppies, but she had an adult female that she'd be willing to sell. I was very apprehensive about bringing an adult into a family with 4 small children, but I agreed to go look at her.

The pet store was a little over an hour away. Once there, the owner told me that the dog was a family pet and she was waiting for her kids to bring her to the store for me to meet. Her daughter entered the store, stating, "Mom, you're not selling Dozer, are you?" Dozer walked in and I squatted down to see her.

All I remember is that she walked right up to me and laid her head in my lap. I was instantly in love. I couldn't believe how affectionate, calm and gentle she was. I knew in my heart that I wanted her and told the lady that I would be back the next day. Looking back, I know that God's hand was on this because I was very foolish. Here I was, bringing home a 50 lb adult Rottweiler in my little Pontiac Grand AM which was packed with myself and my 4 children. Dozie had to sit in the back between my three youngest children with her head resting on the center console between my oldest boy and me.

That night when we got home and got everyone settled in, I remember laying on the floor reading a book to the kids, and Dozie laid down with us to listen. My heart was so full that tears of joy streamed down my face. My family truly felt complete.

I have so many memories of life with her. She went everywhere that we went. She went on walks, fishing and camping with us. She slept in bed with me and helped make me feel less lonely, and I never felt afraid because she was always there. God brought her into my life at such a critical time. And the strange thing is, I didn't even know God at that time. As Matthew 5:45 states, "He (God) causes his sun to rise on the evil and the good, and sends rain on the righteous and the unrighteous." I am always humbled when I consider the many ways that God took care of me even before I loved him. I can't even begin to tell of the stories of his deliverance and providence before I surrendered my life to him.

Another story that I will share is about a time when I had to go to the local food shelf. Thankfully, God gave me a good-paying job that provided well for my family. Because of my income, we didn't receive any public assistance or food support. That being said, I remember one day, feeling overwhelmed with the financial state that my family was in. I broke down sobbing, and pathetically cried out to God, "Why do I have to be so broke? When is it going to get better? I can't even afford cranberry sauce and hot cocoa! What I wouldn't give to have some cranberry sauce and hot cocoa right now" I know it seems ridiculous, but those were comfort foods for me back then. I went to the food shelf, and got my boxes of food, and as I was unpacking, what do you think I found? You guessed it! A can of cranberry sauce and a box of swiss miss hot cocoa packets, with mini marshmallows no less! I too felt in my spirit that God was showing me in a very intimate, personal way, that he sees me and he cares about all the things that I care about.

Now you may be thinking, "well, if God loved you so much, why wouldn't he just change your situation? Arrange it so that you wouldn't be living so broke?" Here's the thing. First of all, we need to have a clear understanding of why there are suffering and sorrows. We have to go back to Genesis 3. We know the story. Satan (through the serpent) tempted Eve to eat of the fruit of the tree which God forbade them to eat from. God gave them everything else in the garden for their enjoyment. It was just this one tree, the tree of knowledge of good and evil that he forbade them to eat from. Satan tempted Eve by causing her to question God's authority, his wisdom, his generosity and his love. He pointed out to her all the alluring aspects of the fruit and the benefits of it to her. Believing that God was withholding some goodness from her, Eve chose to take matters into her own hands. She took and ate of the fruit, then she gave it to her husband, Adam. Instead of assuming the role of leader and protector in their relationship, Adam chose to follow the example of his wife. Because of their poor choices, sin became the reality for humanity. God cursed the serpent, Eve, Adam, and the earth. Just like Eve and Adam, our suffering and sorrows could be a result of our own choices to sin, the result of someone else's choice to sin against us, or just a mere natural occurrence of the world under a curse, such as natural disasters and freak accidents.

James 1:13-15 states "When tempted, no one should say 'God is tempting me'. For God cannot be tempted by evil, nor does he tempt anyone; but each person is tempted when they are dragged away by their own evil desire and enticed. Then, after desire has conceived, it gives birth to sin, and sin, when it is full-grown, gives birth to death." He goes on to say in 4:1-3 "What causes fights and quarrels among you? Don't they come from your desires that battle within you? You desire, but do not have, so you kill. You covet but you cannot get what you want, so you quarrel and fight. You do not have, because you do not ask God. When you do ask, you do not receive, because you ask with wrong motives, that you may spend what you get on your pleasures."

So, you see, as humans, because of our selfishness and sinfulness, we create a lot of problems for ourselves and/or for others. Jesus expresses the seriousness of sin hidden in our hearts in Matthew 5. He states that anyone who harbors anger towards another in their heart is guilty of murder in their heart. Likewise, anyone who indulges in lust after another in their heart is guilty of adultery in their heart. He goes on to say that if your eye causes you to sin, you should cut it out. If your hand causes you to sin, you should cut it off. Now, he's not speaking literally here. He's using hyperbole, which is an extreme exaggeration to make a point. What he's saying is that although we all will face temptation; we have to be aware of what causes us temptation and take drastic measures to avoid falling into temptation. If we don't deal with our hidden sins, we run the risk of eventually acting on them. Even if we don't act on them, indulging in them in our hearts is poison to our soul. Additionally, it is an indictment that we are still sinners because our hearts are not pure. You might argue, "Okay, I can understand suffering from the consequences of my own choices, but still, if God is all-powerful, why doesn't he intervene and rescue me from bearing the consequences of someone else's choices?" Let me assure you, I have asked these questions myself. I am not regurgitating what someone else has taught me. I am sharing with you the things that I've learned through my own wrestling with God over these issues.

When God created Adam and Eve, he created them with free will. He gave them his expectations and the rewards for obedience and the consequences for disobedience, but he did not compel obedience. He allowed them to choose for themselves. He does the same with all of us. Unfortunately, that also means that people have the free will to make choices that are not only sinful against God, but one another as well. God may try to influence us, speaking truth to us about an opportunity to sin, but if we refuse to listen to him, he allows us to go our own way, even if it is to the detriment of ourselves and/or others. The comfort that we have is that God is close to the bro-kenhearted. He hears us when we cry out to him in pain when someone sins against us.

My struggles have taught me things that I probably wouldn't have learned had I not gone through them. I learned that a person really can survive on less. I learned to live minimally which blessed my family greatly. Because we were so broke, most of our family activities were doing things together that were free. We spent a lot of time playing at parks and having picnics. When money was available, I bought things like bikes for each of the kids for their birthdays, fishing rods, and a tent and camping gear. Once these items were bought, we were able to spend a lot of time together as a family enjoying outdoor activities that were virtually free. These activities brought us together through shared experiences that required teamwork.

The abuse that I have suffered has shown me the strength and resilience of the human spirit to overcome. Having faced domestic violence, I am not afraid of death, even less so now that I know that I will be in eternity with Jesus. The sorrows that I've suffered have pushed me into a deeper relationship with my Father, God. I have gained from all this a love and compassion for others that are struggling, but most importantly, I have felt the deep love of my Father in such a real way, that no one can convince me that God does not exist. To me, this is the most priceless gift that I could've been given.

I have lived a life of suffering away from God's friendship. I had chased so many things that the world promised as reliefs for my sorrow. Those things were temporary and left me more empty than what I started with. I needed more and more of whatever I was chasing to achieve the same sense of happiness. My relationship with God, however, has given me hope and joy that is renewed every day.

The apostle Paul writes in 2 Corinthians 1:3-5 "Praise be to the God and Father of our Lord Jesus Christ, the Father of compassion and the God of all comfort, who comforts us in all our troubles, so that we can comfort those in any trouble with the comfort we receive from God." Paul also writes in Romans 5:2-4 "we also glory in our sufferings, because we know that suffering produces perseverance, perseverance character, and character, hope." Jesus' brother James writes in James 1:2-4 "Consider it pure joy, my brothers and sisters, whenever you face trials of many kinds, because you know that the testing of your faith produces perseverance. Let perseverance finish its work so that you may be mature and complete, not lacking anything."

I have also learned more about Jesus through my own sufferings. Jesus was completely blameless. He genuinely loved every person on this earth, yet he was brutalized by the people he loved. What a slap in the face. He loved people so fiercely, and yet, they treated his love like garbage, cruelly abused him then killed him. The interesting thing is that Jesus knew all of this was going to happen to him ahead of time. He knew that he was gonna die for even those who despised and rejected him. He did it anyway. As I've heard it said, "It wasn't the nails that kept Jesus on the cross. It was love that held him there." When I consider Jesus' love for me, it humbles me and moves me to want to learn to love others similarly.

I think our difficulty in loving other people sacrificially comes from the basic fear of our own needs not being met. If we don't believe that our needs will be met -whatever those needs may be- then we can become so determined in having our needs met that we are unable to love others sacrificially.

We need to come to a place where we learn to trust God with our needs and wants for our lives. This can be a very difficult thing to do because we believe that we know what we need and when we need it. To be fair, there are times in our lives that we may truly be in need, such as when I was so broke that I had to go to the food shelf. I can either be angry that God has allowed me to be in a situation where I have to go to the food shelf to receive the food that they give me instead of the foods that I want, or I can be thankful that God enables a food shelf to exist to provide sustenance for my family. Additionally, I consider how I would've missed out on the greatest blessing of seeing the cranberries and cocoa -knowing that God does hear me and cares about even the little things-.

In John 11, Jesus demonstrated this very thing when he received word that his beloved friend, Lazarus was sick and close to death. Instead of immediately dropping what he was doing and making the short trip back to Lazarus and healing him, he stayed where he was for two more days. it is interesting to note that in John 11:5-6 it states (pay attention to this) "Now Jesus loved Martha, and her sister and Lazarus. So, when he heard that Lazarus was sick, he stayed where he was for two more days."

WHAT? Because Jesus loved them, he didn't act immediately? He didn't go to them right away? That seems strange to our minds. Let's read further. Jesus tells his disciples that he's going to Judea. He states (note this) verse 11, "Our friend, Lazarus has fallen asleep; but I am going there to wake him up." His disciples, naturally, took him literally. Verse 12, "Lord, if he sleeps, he will get better." Verse 13 states, "Jesus had been speaking of his death, but his disciples thought he meant natural sleep." Interesting…it seems that Jesus has a different perspective than his disciples. Verse 14 states, "So then he told them plainly, "Lazarus is dead, and for your sake, I am glad I was not there, so that you may believe." Wait! WHAT? Instead of healing Lazarus immediately, he stayed where he was and let him die, because from his perspective it is not death; it's only a nap. And Jesus says he's glad for his disciples' sake that he didn't go immediately to Lazarus so that they may believe?

So, is it possible that Jesus sometimes delays in answering our prayers during our sorrows and suffering because he has a different perspective of our suffering? Is it possible that he intends to do the miraculous in our situation that could only truly be miraculous when it goes against all human logic? Is it possible that sometimes he delays in answering our prayers so that others, too would see and benefit from the miraculous answering of our prayers?

Let's read further. When Jesus arrived in Bethany, it had already been 4 days that Lazarus was in the tomb. Martha ran to meet Jesus and in verse 21 she states, "Lord if you had been here, my brother would not have died". We all have feelings like that, don't we? If Jesus would've just shown up then….

but notice what Martha goes on to say. "But I know that even now God will give you whatever you ask." She still has faith in God's goodness.

Jesus replied to her, "Your brother will rise again."

Martha answered, "I know he will rise again in the resurrection at the last day."

Jesus said to her, "I am the resurrection and the life. The one who believes in me will live, even though they die; and whoever lives by believing in me will never die. Do you believe this?"

Martha responds with, "Yes, Lord, I believe that you are the Messiah, the Son of God, who is to come into the world." Martha had a basic understanding of God's plan of redemption of his remnant people from the teachings of Moses. Living in the time frame that she was, she was living between the two testaments so to speak. Up to that point, all their teachings were from the Old Testament. The Old Testament spoke of the coming Messiah and the resurrection of the remnant on the last day, but Jesus wanted her to understand that he is the Messiah. He is the fulfillment of the Old Testament prophecies. He has power over death. If anyone is to have life after death, they must place their trust in him because he is the Life that defeats death. This lesson was so important for them to learn that he chose to allow Lazarus to die so He Jesus could raise him again, to show all of the people the truth of his power over death.

I love this story because it shows us the truth of Jesus' deity and his humanity. As we read further, in verse 32-33, we see that Mary also comes to Jesus and seeing her and others weeping, he (Jesus) was deeply moved in spirit and troubled. Verse 35 states simply, "Jesus wept." How profound that two-word verse is. As God, Jesus knew how it was all going to turn out. He had no reason for sadness over Lazarus' death. because from his perspective, Lazarus was taking a little siesta. He knew that he was going to raise him again and the girls would have their brother back. Inside, I imagine he was excited like, "Oh girls! I can't wait to show you this!" I could be wrong, but I truly believe that God got excited when he was creating the earth and everything in it. I imagine when he was creating the animals and bringing them to Adam, he was filled with pride and excitement like "Here Adam, what do you think of this one? What are you going to name it?" And especially when he made Eve. Imagine yourself giving a gift to someone. You spent a lot of time making or searching out what you felt was the perfect gift, and you're so excited to give it to that person because you can't wait to see the excitement on their face.

Although Jesus knew Lazarus needed to die to develop and grow the people's faith in him, he felt their pain. Although he knew the good that he intended to bring from this, their sorrow moved him so greatly that he too, wept.

Jesus is not disconnected from our pain, sorrow and suffering. Although he allows it and intends good to come from it, he is with us and he weeps with us. I also find it interesting that Jesus didn't chastise them for lack of faith as in the instances where the disciples were in the boat and afraid of the storm. Instead, he entered their current pain with them.

We know the rest of the story. Jesus tells them to roll away the stone and commands Lazarus to come out. Verse 44 states, "The dead man came out, his hands and feet wrapped with strips of linen, and a cloth around his face."

Although Lazarus was reborn, he was still covered in the burial cloths. I can't help but think of myself. Before Jesus called me from my metaphorical grave, I was dead in my sins. Like a prisoner of sin, my hands and feet seemed bound to evil. My face was covered and I was living in darkness.

Then Jesus said to them, "Take off the grave clothes and let him go." Fascinating, isn't it? Removing the grave clothes that kept me in bondage to sin, gave me freedom.

Verse 45, "Therefore, many of the Jews who had come to visit Mary, and had seen what Jesus did, believed in him." Believing in Jesus meant they too would have everlasting life. In the big scheme of things, having everlasting life with Jesus is much more valuable than a comfortable, sorrow-less, temporary life here on earth. The stakes were high. High enough that Jesus felt that allowing Lazarus to die (and be raised again) was necessary to save many.

Paul helps us put our own suffering into perspective in 2 Corinthians 4:16-18 when he writes, "Therefore, we do not lose heart. Though outwardly we are wasting away, yet inwardly we are being renewed day by day. For our light and momentary troubles are achieving for us an eternal glory that far outweighs them all. So, we fix our eyes not on what is seen, but on what is unseen, since what is seen is temporary, but what is unseen is eternal."

The key is perspective. Being angry and bitter only breeds more anger and bitterness. When we train our minds to consider heavenly perspectives, we can endure suffering with patience, trusting that Jesus has some good planned from it. Either for ourselves, others, or likely, both. That doesn't mean that we must become apathetic in our suffering. As in the story of Martha, Mary and Lazarus, Jesus didn't just understand their sorrow, he entered it with them. All he asked of them was to trust him through it.

A heavenly perspective helps us endure even those little things that aren't related to suffering and sorrow, but rather, inconveniences and annoyances. Learning to be grateful breeds peace and contentment. The apostle Paul writes in his letter to the Philippians, "I know what it is to be in need, and I know what it is to be in plenty. I have learned the secret of being content in any and every situation, whether well fed or in want. I can do all this through him who gives me strength." Philippians 4:12-13.

I believe that the key to achieving contentment is trust in God's providence and his timing. This will require a willingness on our part to consider that in some ways, even our sufferings and the results from them can be viewed as gifts from God. I've also come to know that God's love for me is so deep and immense, that even his answers of "no" to my prayers are an act of protection of me. He knows me better than I know myself and I can trust him to know what is truly best for me.

I pray that if you're struggling right now, that you can feel God's peace descend upon you at this very moment. I pray that you can rest in the knowledge of God's fierce love for you and trust that despite what things look like, he's already working on your behalf.

Heels down, toes up, and chest open. Keep your balance! The trail gets challenging ahead!

Chapter 3

Patience is a Virtue

My dear brothers and sisters, take note of this: Everyone should be quick to listen, slow to speak and slow to become angry, because human anger does not produce the righteousness that God desires.
—James 1:19-20

Life was hard for my children. Even at their tender young ages, they had been through more suffering than any human should. They grew up listening to their father and I argue frequently and witnessed what unrestrained anger can produce. We both were slow to listen to one another. If we listened to one another at all, it was simply to formulate our next rebuttal to the other person's argument. We were quick to speak. We both rushed to argue how the other wasn't meeting our needs and how selfish we viewed the other. We both were quick to get angry. We didn't even like each other, let alone love each other. Maybe your marriage is experiencing similar sorrow, or perhaps you have been close to a couple whose marriage has been in this difficult place.

Neither of us was a believer, so we didn't have the Scriptures to teach us, nor the power of the Holy Spirit to help us. Worse yet, we knew enough about the Scriptures to use them to try to manipulate or coerce the other into doing what we felt they ought to be doing. All we accomplished was driving the other further away. Ecclesiastes 7:9 states, "Do not be quickly provoked in your spirit, for anger settles in the lap of a fool."

Eventually, life became bad enough for all of us, that I decided leaving was necessary. Witnessing violence in the home, going through a divorce, living in separate homes, the constant shuffling back and forth, were all hard on the kids. As if this wasn't bad enough, my children suffered trauma at the daycare they were attending.

One day, in the summer of 2003, I got a phone call from the daycare provider informing me that my youngest child and only daughter, Jenna who was 3 years old at the time, had been run over by a riding lawnmower driven by the daycare provider's 8-year-old son. My children were outside playing when the daycare provider told her 8-year-old son to go mow the lawn. Playing outside, Jenna had run in front of the lawnmower, and the boy panicked, forgetting how to stop the mower, running her over. She was airlifted to Gillette's Children's Hospital in St Paul, MN. When I arrived at the hospital she was still in surgery. I was told that thankfully, the lawnmower only cut up her feet, but that the damage was so extensive that I shouldn't expect for her to ever walk again.

My daughter, who comes from a long line of strong, resilient women, was stubbornly standing with both feet in walking casts in the hospital bed, by the time we were ready to be released from the hospital several weeks later. To this day, my heart breaks each time I think of what they've gone through, and I carry such regret.

About 2 years had passed since Jen's accident when Goldie was born. Jen defied the odds and was running around keeping up with her brothers and this day was no different.

We arrived at Danny and Terry's farm and the kids jumped out of the car as soon as I parked in the driveway. Danny was outside waiting for us. "Can we see the horses, Danny? Please?" They were jumping up and down unable to contain their excitement.

"Yup, they're in the barn with their mamas right now." Danny wasn't even able to finish his sentence when they started running for the barn. Danny, being significantly taller than them, was able to get ahead of them, and stopped them before they could enter the barn. The kids all looked up at him, towering over them. Remaining still, I could tell that they were afraid. "Now hold on there, kids. You can't just rush on in there, like that. You have to move slowly and quietly or you'll scare the horses and you'll get your heads kicked right off," Danny said. "Now listen, you can go in and see them, but you have to listen to me and do what I say. Do you understand?" Danny gently said to them. They nodded their heads and followed his lead.

"Alright, only two can come in the pen with me at a time." Danny took my two oldest boys, Tim and Daniel into the pen where Goldie and Fancy were, first. "Now listen," he whispered, "you have to move slowly, and talk softly or you'll spook them. Horses are big animals and they're scaredy cats. They run away from whatever scares them. If you spook them, they'll turn and knock you over. And look at that big butt," Danny said, pointing to Fancy's rear end. "She'll knock you over without even realizing it." Handing them brushes, he showed them how to brush Goldie and Fancy carefully and quietly.

My two youngest children, Dylan and Jenna were on the outside of the pen watching all of this. "When's it our turn?" Dylan whispered to me, trying desperately to quietly express his impatience.

"Your turn will be soon enough, you little rascal." Danny quietly joked back to Dylan. After a while, Tim and Daniel both got bored and wanted to come out of the pen, so Danny took the brushes and helped them out.

"Alright, you two are next." he said to Dylan and Jen. "Do you remember what I told your brothers?"

"Yup, we're supposed to move slow and be quiet." Dylan said back.

"Good job, young man." Danny said to him. Taking both Dylan and Jen by the hands, he helped them into the pen with Goldie and Fancy.

"You don't have to show us how to brush them; we watched you with Tim and Daniel." Dylan said.

"Alright, show me what ya got hot shot." Danny joked.

I couldn't believe my eyes. It was the cutest thing, seeing Dylan and Jenna brushing Goldie. Goldie was so little they were all almost the same height.

Several times a week, we would go out to Danny and Terry's farm to play with the horses. I couldn't believe the transformation that was taking place in my kids. Spending time with the horses helped them work on speaking quietly and being calm. Danny started assigning the kids more responsibilities like letting them help him grain the horses, or feed them hay and helping by cleaning out the stalls. Danny is a no-nonsense kinda guy, but he's also a gentle giant. Even when he had to get after the kids, he never raised his voice or a hand. We spent so much time out there, that we felt like family. Terry would cook an amazing 4-course meal for all of us. Sometimes, she grilled the meals on their firepit grill. She grew a huge garden and would send vegetables home with us. There was one time when Danny and Dylan got into a water fight using the hose to spray one another. We enjoyed spending time with them. We even helped Danny cut firewood one year. Well, Danny cut the trees down and cut them up into logs that were manageable for us to carry, and we carried the wood to his pickup truck.

To this day, the kids remember, although vaguely, the time that we spent out at Danny and Terry's. I will forever be thankful for their friendship and kindness at such a critical time in our lives. I believe that Danny's presence came at a time that was so important in helping my children heal and grow.

I think we all learned to be a little more calm, patient and kind. It always amazes me when I consider how nervous or anxious energy affects how a person interacts with and interprets the world around them. Conversely, how calm, quiet energy also affects how a person interacts with and interprets the world around them.

A man of knowledge restrains his words and a man of understanding keeps a cool head. —Proverbs 17:27

Being calm, helps a person have a clear mind and more able to listen intently to what someone else is trying to say. Being calm and being "quick to listen and slow to speak" helps you hear more than just the words. You can pause long enough to hear the heart of the person. When dealing with horses, you can listen with your heart and discern the energy of the horse. Is she nervous? Is she frustrated? Scared? Once you have listened to the information, then you can make a better decision based on that information.

Another thing that is so important to learn is that there is no room for anger when working with horses. A horse is so intuitive that she can detect your emotions probably before you can detect your own emotions, and she will react to your emotions before you know what she's reacting to. As it has been said, a horse is your mirror. She will reveal to you what's going on inside of you. Many times, the same is true of people. If you approach conflict with an angry person with anger yourself, many times, it will escalate the conflict. On the other hand, if you approach conflict with peace and calm, it can deescalate the conflict. As Proverbs 15:1 states, "A gentle answer turns away wrath, but a harsh word stirs up anger." I have experienced this in my interactions with many different types of people. Most people just want to be heard. They just want their perspectives, feelings, or opinions validated. Showing them that you care about them, their perspectives and what they're going through is half the battle in de-escalating a conflict. Once the energy and emotions are calmed down, then people are in a better position to use reason and logic in coming up with solutions to problems. Or at the very least, they're in a better position to understand why certain outcomes are not possible at this moment.

Perspective is important. A couple of good questions to ask ourselves are, "What is my ultimate goal in my relationship with this person?" "How will my actions/words at this moment affect the outcome of my ultimate goal?" Again, seeking the wisdom of Proverbs 14:29 states, "A patient man has great understanding, but a quick-tempered man promotes folly." How different and wonderful our world would be if we just took the time to listen to one another with the intent of really understanding the other perspective and without demanding our way.

Chapter 4

I Get by with a Little Help from My Friends

Plans fail for lack of counsel, but with many advisers they succeed.
—Proverbs 15:22

Two weeks after Goldie was born, Willow was born. I fell in love with the idea of having the two sisters, and purchasing Willow also, we named the new little filly "Powers Willow Whiz". Although they were half-sisters, I quickly learned they couldn't have been more different. Goldie was what I called a "compact model". She was short and stout, very sturdy, built like her mama. She was a very curious and friendly little filly, with a calm demeanor and seemed to thrive on human interaction. Willow on the other hand was tall and leggy, long and lean, just like her mama. Her personality seemed to be very high strung and anxious, also just like her mama. Danny told me that Ginger had been abused by her previous owner, and was used only as a broodmare when they purchased her. She was wary of people and seemed to prefer to be left with her herd and content raising babies.

At the time that Goldie and Willow were born, I had only been a born-again Christian for about 6 months. God had done an amazing job in my heart, giving me the desire to turn away from my destructive patterns of coping and instead seek to follow him; however, I hadn't been disciplined to fully submit to all of his leading. Had I been relying on God; I would've been wiser in making decisions. As Proverbs 3:21-23 states, "My son, do not let wisdom and understanding out of your sight, preserve sound judgment and discretion; they will be life for you, an ornament to grace your neck. Then you will go on your way in safety, and your foot will not stumble." I wasn't using sound judgement and discretion when I considered purchasing Willow in addition to Goldie.

All that being said, Willow and I failed to bond. Although I was her owner, ownership didn't equal relationship. Ever since Willow was a little foal, she had an aloof personality. She didn't seek out relationship; in fact, she avoided relationship. She was quite similar to her mother, Ginger.

Because Willow and I failed to bond, we were unable to have a relationship, which in turn made training virtually impossible. it is hard to train a thousand-pound horse to let you get on her back and carry you around everywhere you want to go despite her fears and insecurities. I can't say that I blame her. I think this could be viewed similarly from a spiritual perspective. It's awfully hard to submit to God's training of us if we don't have a relationship of trust with him.

I had taken the knowledge that I gained from when my folks and I trained Brandy, along with what I gained from reading books, watching videos, attending clinics and listening to friends, and set out to training Goldie and Willow, myself. I waited until they were three years old and started just as my parents had. I got them used to a saddle and bridle, and then put my children upon them first, while I led them around. This worked well in desensitizing them to the tack and the idea of people on their backs.

In December 2007, my children and I moved to Bemidji, MN so that I could attend college at Oak Hills Christian college. We lived in the upper level of a duplex on campus. During the first semester, I was fortunate enough to meet a girl who had horses and her own property, and who offered to allow me to board my two girls there. She had shown horses in her youth, so she shared her wealth of knowledge with me and offered to help me train my girls. Because of Goldie's love of people, she and I built an amazing bond which made it relatively easy to train her. She was eager to please and thrived on praise. Willow, on the other hand, proved to be more difficult. She was feisty and her big size intimidated me. I didn't understand her so I couldn't communicate in a way that she could understand me. With Goldie, interacting with her seemed to come naturally to me. Willow bewildered me. I ended up sending her to a trainer, but she continued to intimidate me.

Goldie and I rode frequently with my friend. Through riding together, I grew overconfident and missed a crucial element in building my confidence. I found out later, that my confidence was based on the security of riding with my friend, not with actually having the skills necessary to prove myself a worthy leader. The realization came when my new husband, Tony (whom I married on August 16, 2008) and I moved from Bemidji, MN to Fort Ripley, MN and purchased our own property.

I tried riding Goldie shortly after we moved and she acted like she didn't know anything. It seemed as though she'd forgotten everything that we'd learned while living in Bemidji. I called my friend and asked her for her opinion. She stated that horses sometimes do that when you move. They need time to adjust to the new environment.

Each time that I worked with Goldie, I discovered more and more that I really didn't know what I was doing. I had acquired all these pieces of knowledge over the years (and it was a vast amount of knowledge), but like a large puzzle dumped onto the floor, I sat there looking at all the pieces of knowledge, unsure of how to make it all fit. The harder I tried applying more techniques, the more frustrated I became, and the more frustrated Goldie became.

The wonderful trail rides that we experienced while living in Bemidji were longings of distant past. Now, I was struggling to enjoy just a safe little ride around our yard. I had already fallen off of Goldie at least twice and although I was determined to follow the rule to "get right back on", I was learning that falling off seems to hurt more for a 34-year-old than a 14-year-old.

Why is this so difficult? I moaned. *It wasn't this hard when we trained Brandy. And I had far less knowledge back when we trained her.* I chalked it up to sheer fearlessness in my youth, believing that my fearlessness allowed me the freedom to accomplish whatever I wanted with Brandy.

Then it happened: the day that I almost hung up my hat for good. I mounted Goldie, once again trying to ride. She reared and spun. Trying to get myself readjusted from maintaining balance from her rearing, I was unprepared for what she did next. As soon as her front feet hit the ground, and before I could get settled, she bolted and I fell off. Landing on my right hip, I got hurt pretty badly, physically, psychologically and emotionally.

Once again, Tony was taking me into the emergency room. This time, after several weeks of healing, I was content simply watching the horses in the pasture. It seemed that I had lost my desire for riding. Well, maybe it was more of the fear that I was consumed with eradicated my desire for riding. Over time, little by little, I started to feel desire again. I think there is something true about having "horse" in your DNA. There is no other explanation for the invisible magnetic pull that some of us have for a life with horses. Without a life with horses, we feel empty, or at the very least, "un-whole".

I remember the first day back standing near Goldie after that last accident. I had the intention of making myself get back on her that day. I told myself that my fears were all in my head and that I had to go out with determination and clear intention that I was going to ride today. I was repeating all sorts of affirmations in my head. I began grooming Goldie, and I tacked her up, brought a mounting block up next to her, stepped up onto the mounting block, and then she flinched. My stomach was in my throat, panic consumed me and instinctively, I jumped off the block and said to Tony, "I can't do it. I just can't." So, once again, feeling defeated, I untacked her and took her back out to the pasture where I left my heart and my dreams.

Where no counsel is, the people fall: but in the multitude of counselors there is safety. —Proverbs 11:14

A day or so later, I called Danny, lamenting to him about my plight.

"Kid, ya gotta break it down into smaller steps." He said to me. "Tack her up and start out with lunging her in the round pen. Then, step up on the mounting block. If she moves a single step, lunge her a couple more times. Every time she moves without your permission, lunge her. She'll get the idea that standing still is preferable to running around the round pen. Ya gotta make the right thing easy and the wrong thing hard. Start out with your goal being just sitting on her back. If you can get on her back and just sit there, breathe calmly and let her breathe calmly, consider it a success and call it a day. Ya always gotta end on a good note. That's what she's gonna remember and it'll set the tone for the next day."

So, the next day I put Danny's advice to test. It took a bit, but he was right! I was able to sit on her back that day! I will never forget the lump in my throat when I put my foot into the stirrup, waiting and watching for her to move. She stood still. I took a deep breath and swallowed hard. The moment of truth. I swung my leg over the saddle, carefully, and ready to retract my leg and jump down at the slightest move of a single muscle, but still nothing. I settled into the saddle, still holding my breath, thankful for the watchful eye of Tony right outside the round pen.

"You did it, babe," Tony whispered, excited for me. I soaked it all in, letting my heart relish this moment.

Always end on a good note. I repeated Danny's advice to me in my head. "Better get off now, before something bad happens to ruin it." I said to myself.

Following Danny's advice of breaking everything down into smaller steps, Goldie and I eventually regained the confidence to ride around the yard that summer. However, as is my nature, for good or for bad, I found myself hungering for more. I was elated to be riding again, but I was quickly becoming bored with only being able to tootle around the yard. I concluded that if I was going to be able to ride her off property, I would need to grow in my knowledge and ability and help Goldie grow in her knowledge and abilities. I gobbled up every training book and every DVD I could get my hands on. I read every blog on the internet. I also went to many clinics by different clinicians and eagerly took as detailed notes as I could. The problem with these approaches was that I didn't have a knowledgeable person right there with me to watch me, guide me and correct me when I made mistakes. Truth be told, we couldn't afford to send Goldie to a trainer, and we couldn't afford for me to take lessons. So, our journey is one that is full of different techniques pieced together in our own flavor.

The last missing ingredient was confidence and courage on my part. I had knowledge and skills, now, I just needed to put it to good use and actually DO it.

I have a barn wood sign hanging above our front door inside our house so that you read it as you are leaving the house. It is a quote from John Wayne, saying, *Courage is being scared to death, but saddling up anyway*. I've also heard it said, *Courage isn't the absence of fear, it's pressing on through the fear*. So, I took what I learned from all these different trainers and made my obstacle course at home.

Through repetitively going through the obstacle course at home, it built my confidence, Goldie's confidence and our confidence in each other. We began to KNOW each other. We learned to read each other and develop a consistent way of communicating with each other.

One day, I decided that it was time to try being courageous and take Goldie off the property by myself. I decided ahead of time that if she got dance-y prance-y, that I would try to get her head back on straight and focused on me by practicing some of the skills that we used in the obstacle course at home.

It worked. I was able to ride her a few yards off of the property, and when she started to get anxious, I brought her back to the basics of her training. Things that she knew and was confident in. Being successful in those skills, she calmed down and I figured that was as good a time as any to head back home. While she was still feeling successful. Always end on a good note.

These things are so important for us in our spiritual walks as well. We need other believers to help us grow. Christian artists help us connect with God through their music or their art. Christian scholars and writers teach us through their literature. Christian counselors help by understanding us and helping us to understand ourselves. Learning from a multitude of believers gives us more tools in our toolboxes against sin, but it also helps us have a whole perspective on our personal walks and relationships with God. We only know how far we've come, but others who've gone farther can offer new or different insights that we may not have been able to learn up until this point. Additionally, it is so beneficial belonging to a family of believers who are willing to share one's burdens as well as one's joys as Paul states in Galatians 6:2 and Romans 12:15. The final step is to actually put into practice what we've learned from others. Faith is like a muscle: the more you work it, the stronger it grows.

After giving my life to Jesus, all of the resources that I've mentioned have helped me during times when really hard stuff happened that shook my faith in God. I remember several incidents in which my whole world seemed to be spinning out of control. I couldn't discern truth from lies anymore. I couldn't understand why things were happening and why God would allow these things to happen. Instead of running from God, I went back to what I knew: the basics of my faith. I knew that God is good. There is no evil in him. I knew that God loves me fiercely. I knew that he was with me through all of the sufferings. I knew that he would bring good out of the suffering. Immersing myself in Christian music, literature, art and friendships helped me to continue trusting God. Focusing on those truths -the basics of my faith- helped me find peace in the storm, and they were my anchor until God brought me safely through the storms.

These experiences of facing painful, uncertain circumstances, but trusting

God and him proving himself to be faithful has increased my faith in him.

Consider it pure joy, my brothers and sisters, whenever you face trials of many kinds, because you know that the testing of your faith produces perseverance. Let perseverance finish its work so that you may be mature and complete, not lacking anything. —James 1:2-4

In all this you greatly rejoice, though now, for a little while you may have had to suffer grief in all kinds of trials. These have come so that the proven genuineness of your faith--of greater worth than gold, which perishes even though refined by fire--may result in praise, glory and honor when Jesus Christ is revealed. Though you have not seen him, you love him; and even though you do not see him now, you believe in him and are filled with an inexpressible and glorious joy. —1 Peter 1:6-8

God never wastes our painful experiences; instead, he promises to bring good from the bad if we'll let him. The good that comes brings opportunities to share our lives with others. We are able to enter into the pain and suffering of others because we've been there ourselves. We are able to support and encourage others to continue leaning on Jesus because we have the testimony of deliverance in our own lives.

One of the most beautiful examples that I've seen of devoted friendship comes from Mark 2:3-5. "Some men came, bringing to him (Jesus) a paralyzed man, carried by four of them. Since they could not get him to Jesus because of the crowd, they made an opening in the roof above Jesus by digging through it and then lowered the mat the man was lying on. When Jesus saw their faith, he said to the paralyzed man, "Son, your sins are forgiven."

Sometimes our suffering and sorrow cripple us. We can become paralyzed either emotionally or spiritually (maybe even physically as in the case of major depression) and unable to pursue Jesus on our own strength. We need others to carry us to Jesus. I cannot describe how much comfort has come to me in those times when I've been able to bare my heart honestly with someone and have that person sit with me, take my hand and praying, entreat the Lord of love and compassion on my behalf.

May we all aspire to be those kinds of friends to others and I pray specifically for you, dear reader, that you are surrounded by those kinds of friends. Easy does it. Take some deep breaths, exhale slowly and sit on your pockets. We got a way to go, so we gotta pace ourselves.

Chapter 5

Growing Pains

Because of the Lord's great love we are not consumed, for his compassions never fail; they are new every morning. Great is Your faithfulness. —**Lamentations 3:22-23**

S trangely, these words were written by the prophet Jeremiah, as he looked around at his desolate city. God had warned his people over and over again to turn from their wicked ways and return to him, but they wouldn't listen. Therefore, he found them guilty and sent them off into exile. Yet, Jeremiah had hope. His hope rested in the righteousness, goodness and faithfulness of God. He knew that when God's judgment was complete; he would restore his people. Isn't that a comforting thought? Even if we do things that cause our own suffering, God doesn't just write us off. He doesn't walk away saying, "You made your bed, you lie in it." He promises that when we repent, he will restore us at the right time.

As I mentioned earlier, I didn't know how to work with Willow, because she was so very different from Goldie. I tried. I read from as many different trainers' books as I could get my hands on. I tried as many different techniques as I could. We both were becoming more and more frustrated and more and more resentful of one another.

I decided that for both of our sake, it was time to sell Willow. Perhaps someone else could work with her. So, I advertised her for sale on the internet and that's how Kelee and I met.

The day before Kelee was going to come look at her, Willow had become so unpredictable that I considered her dangerous. I had had enough of her. I sent Kelee a message and told her that there was no point in coming to see her. I was sending her to auction because she simply was too dangerous. Kelee tried to dissuade me by telling me that she would only go to slaughter. I replied that I didn't care, for as dangerous as she was acting, maybe that was what was best. Kelee begged me to just allow her to come and look at her first. Hesitantly, I agreed, but I told her that under no conditions would I allow her to attempt to ride her. Kelee agreed and we kept the arrangement to meet the next day.

Kelee came out the next day with a friend. We walked out to the pasture and I gave Kelee the halter and lead rope. I told her that Willow had gotten to the point that she wouldn't let me catch her. Perhaps, Kelee being someone different could catch her. I stood off at a distance, watching from my peripheral vision. I couldn't believe it. Willow walked right up to Kelee! As Kelee approached us, I exclaimed, "If I didn't know any better, I would think that God wanted you to have her!"

Kelee took Willow to the round pen and began free lunging her as I stood along the outside, watching with her friend. What I witnessed next, was a true miracle. I watched Kelee directing Willow in the round pen, then Kelee turned her back and immediately, Willow stopped then turned and walked straight up to Kelee. At first, I was scared for Kelee's safety because she had turned her back to Willow. I didn't know what to think. I knew absolutely nothing about Kelee. I didn't know her level of horse experience, but there was something about her…I held my breath and chose to trust that Kelee knew what she was doing. I couldn't believe what happened next. Willow walked right up to Kelee's back and rested her head on Kelee's shoulder. It was as if time stood still. I swear every one of us held our breaths in unbelief. Tears filled my eyes. I knew that God was telling me that Willow needed to go with Kelee.

Kelee had seen enough and said that she would like to buy Willow if I would let her. I was still concerned, so I asked that she sign a paper stating that she was fully aware of all the behavioral issues that Willow has and that she releases me and my family of any liability of any accidents that may arise from riding Willow.

I had no idea what price to put on Willow, as I was at the point of being willing to sell her even at slaughter price. So, I gave her and her friend privacy as they discussed what they felt was a fair price. I prayed, "Lord, you know what is fair for everyone involved. You set the price. I will accept whatever they offer because I know that the price is coming from you."

A month after Kelee had Willow settled in the boarding facility, she wrote to me and told me how much Willow had come to mean to her. I won't tell her story, because it is her story to tell, but suffice it to say that Willow had given her renewed hope in God. There's is a story of horse and girl saving one another.

Kelee and I grew to be good friends and I got to watch the transformation that God had done in both of them. Through love, trust, respect, and knowledge, Kelee was able to provide the proper discipline for Willow and trained her to be a reliable, faithful mount Discipline and punishment are not equal. According to dictionary.com, *Punishment* is *the infliction or imposition of a penalty as retribution for an offense. Discipline,* on the other hand, is *the practice of training another to obey rules or a code of behavior, using punishment to correct disobedience.* When we use punishment (whether on horses, children or even adults under our leadership) without having first provided the instruction (discipline), punishment becomes unfair, unreasonable, and perhaps even cruel, especially if punishment is carried out in anger.

In your anger do not sin, do not let the sun go down while you are still angry, and do not give the devil a foothold. —Ephesians 4:26-27

Anger is a natural human emotion; however, God tells us that we have to control it and remove it from our hearts daily, or Satan will use it to control us. Unrestrained anger can have devastating and even dangerous results. Discipline has the goal of teaching, using consequences (punishment) as necessary. Through discipline, Kelee was able to teach Willow and change her behavior and thereby, saving her life.

Over the next year or so, Kelee purchased more horses and started a horse-riding business, giving lessons to kids. It turned out that Kelee was quite the accomplished horsewoman even in her early 20's. The most beautiful thing I got to witness was a bond being formed between Willow and Kelee. I didn't believe it was possible, but the evidence was in the pictures and the videos. Willow loved Kelee and Kelee loved her. My heart was so happy that Willow finally got to experience love. However, more surprises were to come. Kelee had pictures of Willow even being used as a lesson horse for inexperienced riders. I couldn't believe my eyes. Several years later, Willow even got to experience the love of being a mother when she gave birth to her first foal. Sadly, in 2018, Willow passed away from a severe case of colic. I will forever be thankful to God for putting Kelee in our paths and giving Willow the chance to love and be loved.

My foolishness and hasty decision to buy Willow, and my lack of experience in training her contributed to the problems between us. Because I failed in communicating appropriately with her, she developed behavioral issues which ultimately lead to dangerous situations. However, God in his wisdom, arranged to bring Kelee and Willow together so that, together, he saved both of their lives.

As our Creator, God is entitled to ownership of our lives. However, he knows that ownership does not equal relationship, and that is what he desires: a personal, intimate relationship with each of us. A relationship in which we can walk together and talk together, and journey life together.

God allows us to go through impossible circumstances to prove that nothing is impossible for him (Luke 18:27). He wants us to believe that his power is perfect in our weakness (2 Corinthians 12:9). Our faith shouldn't be in our own knowledge, skills, abilities, finances, popularity, etc, because at any given time those things won't be enough. Confronting an obstacle that we have absolutely no power to overcome, can devastate us and leaves us vulnerable to harmful and self-destructive alternatives.

I think many of us have developed behavioral problems that led us far from God, not because God is inept at knowing how to communicate and relate to us, but because of our own rebellious hearts Sometimes our rebellion takes us into unsafe places where we suffer abuses at the hands of others. Sometimes our rebellion causes suffering to others. God, as our loving Father, tries to discipline us and get us onto the correct path, however, as had been my case those many years before completely surrendering my life to Jesus, if we continue to stubbornly rebel, he chooses to chasten us, even severely, rather than let us destroy ourselves and/or others

Deuteronomy 8:5 says, "Know then in your heart, that as a man disciplines his son, so the Lord God disciplines you." Job 5:17 says, "Blessed is the one whom God corrects; so, do not despise the discipline of the Almighty." Proverbs 3:12 says, "because the Lord disciplines those he loves, as a father the son he delights in." Hebrews 12:11, "No discipline seems pleasant at the time, but painful. Later on, however, it produces a harvest of righteousness and peace for those who have been trained by it." Job 8:4 says, "When your children sinned against him (God) he gave them over to the penalty of their sin." As noted by Romans 1:21-32, in extreme cases where we absolutely refuse his chastening, he allows us to go our own way, and suffer the consequences of a world much harsher than himself. He chastens us in love while the world chastens us mercilessly. However, even in the chastening, God never leaves us or forsakes us. When we decide to surrender to his correction, he is quick to receive us. He repairs the damage done to ourselves and others and gives us new blessings of a hopeful future. When we choose to trust God in impossible circumstances, it allows him to deliver us and prove himself faithful, thereby increasing our faith in him, then, that faith in him becomes an anchor for our souls in future circumstances.

Where are you at, friend? How are you doing? Are you experiencing peace at the moment? Or does your life feel chaotic and overwhelming? Instead of allowing anxiety and worry to propel us into a frenzied attempt to control our situations, or instead of pursuing destructive alternatives that only make our situations worse, we can take a deep breath crying out to God, and courageously wait to see how he rescues us.

Sometimes God removes the impossible circumstance, sometimes money just happens to fall into our hands, (yes, this has actually happened to me on several different occasions!) sometimes God uses people who just happen to say or do just the thing that we need at that moment, and sometimes God even uses animals.

Easy now. We're gonna slow down a bit, so loosen your reins and admire the beauty around you.

Chapter 6

Trailer Woes

So do not fear, for I am with you; Do not be dismayed, for I am your God. I will strengthen you and help you. I will uphold you with my righteous right hand. —Isaiah 41:10

Can you think of a time in your life when you were afraid? What was that like for you? How did you handle it? One of the most stressful experiences that I've had in my horse hobby, was hauling my horse on a major highway, several hours away from home all by myself. One of my biggest horse-related fears is the act of trailering the horses away from home. Especially long distances away from anyone who can help. So many things can go wrong. The worst-case scenario is a wreck in which everyone dies. The least case scenario is that I get a flat tire and have to call roadside assistance to come and change it. I'll never forget the day I sold Willow to Kelee, who lived several hours away. She didn't have transportation to haul Willow to the barn that she was planning on boarding her at, so I naively agreed to transport her. I thought to myself, "How hard could this be? I'm used to driving in the cities." For the record, my travels in the cities did NOT include a horse trailer and horses.

I soon found out that transporting a living animal in a stock trailer in 4 lane traffic, near the cities, is not for me. I checked all the lights on the trailer and loaded Willow early that morning. I tried to plan my driving time in a way to avoid the rush hour traffic. That's hard to do when it seems like at every hour near the cities there is rush hour traffic. I've traveled several hours with the horses before, but that was in north-central MN on relatively quiet roads. Additionally, I had the security of Tony following me in case anything went wrong. This time would be different, Kelee would be ahead of me, leading the way. The ride started well and uneventful. I was feeling confident and relaxed. Although I hadn't had much experience hauling horses, the experiences that I had up to that point, were all good so I had no point of reference for fear. That was going to change during "city" traffic. Traveling to the cities in the past, I always kept myself in one of the middle lanes so that I would have fewer chances of being surprised by left or right lanes suddenly changing into off-ramp lanes. Being in the center lanes also gave me more ability to change lanes slower. I would keep my eyes fixed on the green directional signs on the overpass bridges ahead of me. This time, I was completely dependent on following Kelee's lead. I had no idea where we were going, so I had to keep Kelee in my view at all times. This in itself was difficult in the traffic that we were in. Cars were going a minimum of 70 mph and were weaving in and out between Kelee and I. Keeping Willow safe and changing lanes slowly was my highest priority, which meant that I was driving slower than the traffic around me and I allowed many people to pass and get in front of me. This created a problem because it interfered with my ability to follow Kelee and change lanes with her.

Most people don't understand what driving a stock trailer is like, let alone a loaded trailer with precious cargo. it is difficult to stop quickly because the trailer itself is several thousand pounds, in addition to a 1200-pound living animal inside. Changing lanes quickly is also difficult. I like to make sure that the trailer is moving fluidly with the truck to avoid causing my horse to lose her balance. A horse losing her balance can create a dangerous situation at worst, at the very least, it could cause a horse to develop a fear of traveling.

A car switched lanes, darting right in front of me. I was traveling too fast, and there was too much weight for me to be able to slow down quickly enough to maintain a safe distance between him and us. I knew that I couldn't slam on the brakes because I was traveling too fast and it would cause Willow to slam into the front of the trailer. Quickly, I scanned my surroundings, assessing the best course of immediate action. There was no other option than to change into the left lane. I switched lanes quickly to avoid slamming into the rear end of the car ahead of me. However, I felt Willow lose her balance and heard a loud thud coming from the trailer. I felt the back end of the trailer swerve and the I felt the truck pulling back. The trailer swerved again, slightly and then we were safely aligned.

I was really shaken up and was worried about Willow. I glanced back through the rearview mirror and could see her through the window of the trailer. I was able to see her head and her rump so I knew that she was still standing upright. I then scanned ahead to try to locate Kelee's car. She was already in the far right lane getting ready to exit onto the off-ramp. I quickly glanced through my side mirrors to check to see if I was clear to merge right. I saw an opening and immediately turned my signal on and began merging right. The cars were far enough behind me that I was able to merge slowly and safely. I began merging far enough ahead, that the cars behind me had enough time to adjust their speeds so I took my time merging to move fluidly for Willow's sake.

Once off the freeway, we were able to get to the boarding stable where Willow would be boarded without further incidence. We arrived and let Willow relax before opening up the trailer and unloading her.

After showing me around the barn, Kelee and I returned to the trailer to unload Willow and assess her for any injuries. There were no apparent injuries, but she seemed still shaken up from the ride. We unloaded her and Kelee took her to a round pen to let her walk around on the solid ground. I went inside the trailer and noticed that there was a small concave spot between the floor and the wall where the side had bent away from the floor. I could only guess that this was related to the bang I heard. I shuddered at the thought of how bad things could've gone.

I said goodbye to Willow and Kelee, then I began the long ride back home. I only made it a couple of miles down the road when I felt a pull coming from the trailer. I checked my left mirror and saw that I had a flat tire on the trailer. I couldn't believe my luck. Calling our roadside assistance, I noticed that my cell phone battery was nearly drained and I realized that I didn't have a car charger with me. I began to panic, wondering if I'd have enough battery to complete the call and get help. I also realized that since I'd followed Kelee down here, I wasn't confident on how to get us back home. It wasn't likely that I'd have enough battery to use my GPS to get at least to a familiar area. I couldn't believe how bad this trip was going.

The tow truck arrived and told me that it was fortunate that the trailer was unloaded because they don't perform any assistance on a loaded trailer. I thanked God that he ensured that I got Willow to the barn before the tire blew. I also thanked him that the tire blew on this lonely country road instead of the freeway. I became physically sick thinking of what it would've been like had the tire blown on the freeway. I turned off my phone, hoping that the battery would recharge itself and sat inside the truck trying to figure out what I was going to do, while the guy changed out the trailer tire.

After the tire was changed, I began trying to make my way back home. I took a road that I thought looked familiar, however, after a short distance, it was evident that this was the wrong road and it was starting to get dark. I had to figure out how to turn the trailer around. When I practised at home, I was able to back the trailer up but only in our yard, where I had lots of room to maneuver. Truth be told, I wasn't even good at it at home. I preferred to use as much space as necessary for just making a wide circle, avoiding backing entirely.

After what seemed like an eternity with a lot of maneuvering, I was able to get turned around and back on the road I came from. I was getting physically sick at this point. I prayed that God would give me the memory that I needed to get on the right road, at least until I got further north in a familiar area. I turned my cell phone back on just to see if the battery recharged at all. It had. However, just the act of turning it on began draining what little charge it gained. I quickly entered my map app and put in the address for home. I checked the directions and memorized the first few steps at least to get on the right track before the battery went dead. Then I turned my phone back off so that I would be able to use it in case of emergencies.

Thankfully, God answered my prayer and brought to mind roads that I had traveled down. Once I reached the freeway, I was able to follow the signs that took me back home.

I wish that my spiritual walk with God had those obvious, big, green signs to lead me where I need to go. That's why it is so important for me to stay immersed in the Scriptures. As the psalmist writes in Psalm 119:105, "Your word is a lamp to my feet, and a light on my path." Typical lamps in those days were just little lanterns filled with oil and a wick. They probably illuminated only a few feet circumference. The illumination of one of these ancients' lamps seems an appropriate image for certain times in my faith walk. I can't count how many times I've been going a certain way, only to have suffering and sorrow detour me. Confused about the circumstances, I have had difficulty discerning what to do next. Paralyzed with fear and neurotic about making the wrong decision, I've allowed myself to stay stuck for longer than I should've.

In the earlier years of my life, when I was living a life of just trying to survive, I developed conditioned responses to fear. These conditioned responses became so ingrained in me that my body began responding to any stress as though I was in a life-threatening situation. For almost a decade after being free from physical abuse, I was still held captive to the fear in my past.

Where are you, friend? Are you struggling as I have? Are you unsure of the direction to go in? Does fear have you stuck?

When I make myself sit quietly long enough, I hear the still small voice of the Lord telling me, *Just take one step. That's all you need to do. Take one step of faith, show one act of love, forgive one offense, withhold one unkind remark. Just start with one. Then another.* Slowly, one by one, the journey resumes and as I look back, I learn more about myself and God, who loves me. Isaiah 58:11 states, "The Lord will guide you always; he will satisfy your needs in a sun-scorched land and strengthen your frame."

I learned a lot from that day taking Willow through the cities. I learned that I really need to learn how to maneuver the trailer better and learn how to change trailer tires myself. I learned to keep a cell phone charger on me at all times, and that it would help if I printed off the directions before leaving. I learned that I'd like to trade my stock trailer in for a nice, padded slant load; but I digress... I learned that just as I followed Kelee so meticulously, I need to keep my eyes as diligently on God. Although he may allow me to go through stressful events, he is always with me. I just need to calm down enough to hear him and follow his direction. As the psalmist says in Psalm 18:30, "As for God, his way is perfect: The Lord's word is flawless; he shields all who take refuge in him." Just as he prevented the tire from going flat on the freeway and while Willow was in the trailer, God also shields me from other stresses and sufferings.

Struggling with an anxiety disorder for decades, it's hard for me to not worry. However, as I trust God more and more, I can look back and see how much I've grown. I still struggle, but I don't struggle as frequently or intensely as I used to. I'm finding that the key is in learning to rest in his promises that he will strengthen me and uphold me and that he is always with me. By becoming trained in listening to God's truth in each situation, instead of passively allowing our bodies to react to stressful situations, we can become free from the bondage of fear

Isaiah 42:16 states, "I (God) will lead the blind along ways they have not known, along unfamiliar paths I will guide them; I will turn the darkness into light before them and make the rough places smooth. These are the things I will do; I will not forsake them." What an encouraging promise that is!

Chapter 7

We've Got a Trail to Blaze

Teach me to do your will, for you are my God; May your good Spirit lead me on level ground. —Psalm 143:10

Learning to do God's will. Does that conjure up negative emotions inside of you? Do you feel like you're choking under the weight of what feels like impossible expectation? That's how I felt before I understood God's grace. When we read the Bible there seems to be a lot of "do's" and "don'ts" and it feels overwhelming. Like how can anybody live up to all that? The good news of the Gospel is that God loves us so much that he decided to come to earth in the form of a human -Jesus- to help us out

Jesus (God in the flesh) was the only perfect person who's ever walked the earth; therefore, his life was the only sacrifice that would pay the debt of humanity's sins. He gave up his life to cancel the debt we owed and when we meditate on the cruelty of his death, it moves us to understand just how deep his love is for us. But that's not the end of the story.

As God, he also has power over death, and three days after his death, he rose again. This assures us that with death defeated, we, too, will rise again. However, that also is not the end of the story. After Jesus ascended to heaven, the Holy Spirit was sent to live in the hearts of every person who personally accepts Jesus' sacrifice for the payment of their sins. This is the exciting part. So, any person who has the Spirit living inside of them has the power to do God's will. Instead of following a rule book, we begin to read the Bible as God's user manual for our lives. It isn't a matter of "what should I do" or "shouldn't do", but rather, "what shows God that I love him and what shows that I love others like myself"? We aren't accountable to other humans' (even other Christians') lists of "do's" and "don'ts" rather, we are listening and obedient to God, himself, and his direction.

The more that we spend time with God, reading his Word, asking him to explain it to us, and listening for the answer, the more sensitive we'll become to the Spirit's leading.

The key to every life door is love. If you love God with everything you have; your heart, soul, strength, and mind, God considers you his friend and he reveals all things to his friends -albeit in his timing- when he knows that we have the ability to understand. John 15:15

Following God's lead isn't easy, but God promises to never leave us or abandon us, so even if he leads us through some scary situations, he is always with us every step of the way.

Tony and I had met in 2001 through work at the same state-operated group home that Danny and I worked at. Several of us staff had become good friends, and even after all of these years, we still stay in touch. Tony and I had known each other for nearly eight years when he proposed to me in May of 2008. We married on August 16, 2008, and had been married for almost four years when we began looking seriously for a horse for him.

Goldie and I were making great progress riding around our yard. I had made games for us to have fun with, like weaving in and out of our many trees in our yard, weaving in and out of poles that I had erected with orange safety cones, carrying rings and slipping them over the poles as we walk around them, walking around barrels, playing polo with brooms and inflated plastic balls, and basketball, where someone would hold a hula hoop and we'd ride by and toss the ball into the hoop. Yes, Goldie and I were re-building our bond and growing in our trust and enjoyment of each other, but I wanted to be able to ride trails and even better, to do it with my other best friend, my husband.

Tony was an even more of an inexperienced rider than myself, so he needed a special horse. A horse that people have come to refer to as a "husband horse" or "baby sitter" or more commonly known as "bomb proof".

I had been searching the internet for weeks now and had already looked at several horses. None of them seemed to strike me as "the one". Then, one day I discovered an advertisement for an Appaloosa, named Blaze. Upon arriving at the barn where Blaze was boarded, Ellen greeted me with a warm, friendly smile; she was his owner. She explained to me that she had owned Blaze since he was a baby and had trained him herself. His list of capabilities and experiences was longer than my arm. Her smile quickly disappeared as she sadly explained to me that some conflicts in her boarding and living situation were necessitating his sale.

Ellen introduced me to Blaze. He was all white with the only hint of Appy markings visible as mottling around his eyes and muzzle. "Why the name, 'Blaze'?" I wondered to myself. "He's as white as snow."

He was a tall horse and despite what Ellen told me about him being bullied by the other horses making him "the bottom of the pecking order" in the herd, he held his head high and proud. She took him out and rode him in the outdoor arena to show me everything that he could do. After bringing him back, I asked her if I could try him out. I signed the barn's release of liability and got on him. Immediately, I felt my stomach in my throat and recognized panic rising within me. All those old fears came rushing back to me. It didn't help that he was quite a bit bigger than Goldie. I didn't want to look like a complete fool to Ellen, so I tried to put on a poker face and appear confident. I rode him around the outdoor arena at a walk. I tried to put him into a trot, but only managed a couple of strides before quickly bringing him back to a walk.

"He seems like a good boy," I said to her. She beamed with pride. "I have a couple of other horses to look at before I make a decision. How soon do you need an answer?" I asked.

"I need to be moved in a couple of weeks, so the sooner the better." She stated, again, her smile dropping.

"Ok, I'll be in touch." I said as I entered my truck. I already had my mind made up. I did not want this horse. Honestly, I couldn't deny that I was intimidated by him. I didn't know why. He didn't do anything that I perceived as threatening. In fact, he was perfect, so I couldn't understand where my insecurities were coming from. I just felt like he was too advanced for me. I was looking for a horse for a beginner. A horse that anyone with little to no horse sense could get on and the horse, being so well trained, would just walk along, taking care of its inexperienced rider. Remembering the glint in his eyes, and the proud way he held his head, Blaze just didn't seem like that type of horse. Discouraged and putting the idea out of my head, I drove home resigned to continue my quest.

A week had gone by and I was no closer to finding our perfect saddle pal than when I had started. I had exhausted nearly every horse sales site on the internet and was becoming bored from checking them every day (sometimes several times per day). My phone rang. I looked down at the caller ID. It was Ellen. I groaned. "Ugh, what am I gonna tell her? How am I gonna tell her that I'm just not interested?" I forced a smile as I answered the call. "Hello?"

"Hi, Kandy?" Ellen asked when I answered.

"Yup, this is she." I stated.

"This is Ellen, Blaze's owner."

"Oh, hey, Ellen, how are you?" I asked.

"Oh, I'm fine. I was just wondering if you'd made your decision about Blaze."

My heart pounded. *I hate having to tell people 'no'*, I said to myself. I took a deep breath.

"I thought about it, and I just don't think he's a good fit for us." I blurted out, trying to sound as apologetic as I could. Silence on the other end. I felt absolutely terrible.

"I need to tell you something," Ellen replied. "I hope this doesn't sound crazy, but I believe God is telling me that he's supposed to go to you."

"What?" I thought in my mind. I have what I consider a pretty close relationship with God, myself. I rely on his wisdom on nearly everything that I do, and I haven't heard him tell me that Blaze is supposed to go to me. Of course, being honest, I had to admit that this was one of those times that I hadn't actually been praying and listening to God about which horse was right for us. "Well." I started. "How much are you asking for him?"

"seven hundred-fifty dollars for him. And I'll include all of his tack."

I just about choked. I knew that although he wasn't registered, a horse of his ability and training was worth several thousand dollars. Not counting his tack, his saddle alone, was probably worth at least five hundred dollars "Ok, I'll talk it over with my husband and get back to you later today." I replied.

"Sounds great! Talk to you soon." I hung up the phone, stunned at what was transpiring. When Tony got home, I told him the strange story.

"So how low do you think she'll go?" He asked me. Tony never gave anyone what their asking price is. It's like an exhilarating challenge for him to negotiate with people.

"I am not going to negotiate her price!" I exclaimed. "Seriously? It's unreasonable for her to sell him AND all his tack at such a low price as it is!"

"Alright, It's your call." Tony said to me.

I dialed Ellen's number. "Hello, Ellen? I'll be down tomorrow to get Blaze."

"Sounds great. I'll see you tomorrow, then." She answered.

Then I went outside and got busy setting up a quarantine pasture for him. *Boy, I hope God told Blaze and Goldie that Blaze is supposed to come to us.* I thought to myself as I lay down in bed that night.

It was an understandably emotional event for Ellen. I actually suggested that she keep him because I saw how broken her heart was as we loaded him into the trailer.

"No, no. I have to move and where I'm moving, I can't have him. No, he needs to go with you", she assured me, albeit sadly.

"Let's be Facebook friends." I suggested. "That way we can stay in touch and you can stay updated on how he's doing."

"I would really love that", she said.

The ride home was, thankfully, uneventful. We pulled into the yard, and immediately Goldie and Blaze began whinnying. I'm sure they must've smelled each other and were vocalizing their curiosity. We got Blaze out of the trailer and took him to his pasture adjacent to Goldie's. We wanted them to have the opportunity to get to know each other over the fence before putting them together. Goldie was used to being lead mare in every herd that she'd been in. So, when Blaze ran to investigate his new pasture pal, Goldie ran the fence line snorting and kicking and striking her feet. She would approach the fence where Blaze was standing, and he'd stretch his neck over the fence in an attempt to say *Hello*, but Goldie would squeal and strike the ground in front of them. Blaze looked at her as if she was deranged.

"Ummm…." Tony started. "I don't think God gave Goldie the memo."

"Yeah. This will be interesting." I agreed. "I guess we'll just keep 'em separated until Goldie calms down."

Ellen had told me that the best thing for Blaze once we get him home, is to get riding him as soon as possible. "He knows his job, and it's really important for him to get to work as soon as possible after being moved. That way he doesn't get lazy and develop bad habits." She had said to me.

"Ok, buddy." I said to him a couple of days after getting him home. "I got a job for you. We're gonna go for a ride." I tacked him up and got up on him. Tony was standing nearby. "Alright, buddy, let's go." I said, squeezing him and then clucking.

He planted his feet and refused to move. I started to feel that familiar nervousness setting in. *Oh, no.* I thought to myself. *Come on, buddy.* I squeezed harder and clucked again. His head sprung up and his ears darted forward. I felt his body tense up. Immediately, I jumped down, and began crying to my husband, "I can't do this. I just can't."

"Babe. He didn't do anything." Tony said to me.

"I know, but it felt so much like Goldie, just before she'd freak out on me." I cried. Tony sighed a deep sigh. I could sense the disappointment.

"Listen." He said to me. "I know that you've had some bad experiences, but these horses aren't cheap and I'm not gonna pay for a bunch of pasture pals. Either you figure it out and get riding again, or we're gonna sell them." I knew he was right.

As harsh as it sounded, we both knew that it needed to be said. I needed the kick in the pants to either cowgirl up or sell the horses. I called the neighborhood girl and asked her if she was interested in going for a ride with me. "I bought a new gelding and I wanna try him out to see how he does, but I'm afraid to go out by myself." I explained to her.

"Sure, I'll come over and we can ride down to my brother's house." She suggested.

I admired her. Although she was still in high school, she possessed horse knowledge, skill, and experience that I was envious of. Her mare was a stocky paint horse and very well trained in dressage. It didn't take too long before I saw the both of them making their way to our house. Tony helped me to get back on Blaze and her and I trod down our driveway onto the road to her brother's house. However, before long the sky started to turn black and the wind picked up.

"Oh, no," I muttered under my breath. "You've got to be kidding me. Nice. A storm. Just perfect for my first ride on him."

"It'll be ok," the cheerful neighborhood girl assured me. "We'll hunker down in the barn until the storm passes."

The wind continued to pick up, and the rain started coming down. I could hear thunder in the distance and lightning flashed. Blaze didn't flinch a muscle. He put his head down and pressed on through the rain. The rain continued to come down in sheets and the thunder and lightning continued to advance closer when we finally made it to the house. The neighborhood girl got off of her horse and opened the barn doors for us to stand in the doorway. We all were soaked as we stood in the doorway feeling the ground shake from the thunder and watching the lightning flash around us. I nervously watched Blaze's reactions. There was none. At least none that I could see. He stood there, steady as a rock. I was humbled by his courage and sat in awe of his calmness.

"Yay!" The girl beamed, snapping me back to attention to her. "The storm is passing. We can head back now."

We emerged from the barn, and she closed the doors and remounted. The sky was still a deep blue color, but the wind was dying down, the sheets of rain subsided to light sprinkles, and we slowly made our way back home. Along the way, another neighbor drove by honking his horn and waving at us. My body became tense, and I felt panic rising inside of me, waiting for Blaze to explode in fear, himself. I couldn't believe how he just calmly walked on without so much as a flinch.

By the time we approached our driveway, Tony and the neighborhood girl's mom were waiting and watching for us. Tony had a concerned look on his face. The sun was starting to peek out from the clouds and the faint colors of a rainbow appeared just when I strode directly in front of Tony.

"I got pretty worried once that storm blew in." He said. "I couldn't believe how fast it moved in!"

"Sooo…How'd he do?" Tony asked me, eyeing me carefully, unable to hide the anticipation in his voice.

Excitement filled my heart. For the first time in a long time, I felt hopeful excitement. Taking a moment to reflect on what just happened, how Blaze took charge and took care of me, I was overwhelmed with emotion. Grinning from ear to ear, drenched and dripping from head to toe, I looked at Tony and gushed, "It was so freaking awesome!" I dismounted and wrapped my arms around Blaze. "Thank you so much!" I whispered into his neck.

Gazing up at this beautiful, white, yes, Appaloosa, who was leading me safely through my fears, I realized that Blaze was indeed the perfect name for him.

God promised to send the Holy Spirit to help us follow him (Ezekiel 36:27). Jesus also told us that once he died and ascended into heaven, only then would the Holy Spirit be sent to live within us as our guide (John 14). The Holy Spirit living within believers in Jesus Christ, functions much the same way that Blaze did for me that day. To be honest, I truly believe that some horses are gifted in knowing that they have an inexperienced rider on their back and they take care of them. Those horses are so special and worth their weight in gold.

We don't have to be afraid of following the leading of the Holy Spirit. Being the third person of the Trinity, he is God, so he knows everything and how it will all turn out. The only requirement of us is belief in him that he can do it (Matthew 13:58).

We can truly begin living a life of excitement rather than one of fear when we learn to trust the leading of the Holy Spirit. We can be assured that he will guide us safely through whatever storms we will face. Depending on him to get us through the storms of life creates spiritual confidence within us. I was exhilarated, realizing that I had survived that terrifying thunderstorm, and I was humbled and thankful to Blaze for taking care of me. That experience was the bedrock for trusting him enough to try new things because I knew what he was capable of. The same thing happens in our faith walk with God.

Like Peter in Matthew 14:28-30, stepping out of the boat to walk to Jesus, we must step out in faith, following the Spirit's leading, because it is essential for growth in our trust. Also, like Peter, we must keep our eyes on Jesus. When Peter, saw the wind, he got concerned, that's when he started to sink. Then he panicked. Then he cried out to Jesus to save him. We too will face many storms that threaten to shipwreck and drown us. Those storms will seem so terrifying that they can have the power to drive us to complete despair.

The only way to survive those spiritual storms is by having a spiritual lighthouse guiding us to shore. That lighthouse is the Holy Spirit, but we have to have a bedrock of trust established during little storms, in order to give us the confidence to trust him to guide us through the devastating ones. The author of Hebrews writes in Hebrews 12:1-3, "Therefore, since we are surrounded by such a great cloud of witnesses, let us throw off everything that hinders and the sin that so easily entangles, And let us run with perseverance the race marked out for us, fixing our eyes on Jesus, the pioneer and perfecter of faith. For the joy set before him he endured the cross, scorning its shame, and sat down at the right hand of the throne of God. Consider him who endured such opposition from sinners, so that you will not grow weary and lose heart."

Yes, we have to be aware of the things going on around us and we have to be wise in avoiding danger, but we can't focus on those things. If we pay too much attention to the potential dangers, our minds can become overwhelmed and we begin to be weighed down by panic. Our emotions which become a hindrance to us need to be thrown off. Being preoccupied with the cares and worries of the world seems noble according to the world's standards, however, according to God's standards, it can be a form of idolatry. Idolatry is a sin that easily entangles and must be thrown off. Notice that the writer doesn't say "lay aside" or "lay down". He states that we are to "throw off", as with intention, determination and force. We must run with perseverance, but who can win a marathon before training to run it? Perseverance in the suffering sprints helps us build endurance in running the suffering marathons. Keeping our eyes on Jesus gives us the visual example of how to run the race effectively. By his example, we learn that because of our rewards in eternity, we can endure our present suffering without shame.

No matter how bad things look, no matter what the perceptions are of others, we can endure because we know that Jesus is on our side. And where is he seated? At the right hand of God. He is sitting in a place of authority and power to save and reward us. Additionally, when we consider all that he endured at the hands of sinners, it enables us with strength and courage to follow in his footsteps.

If you're in a place right now, where you feel overwhelmed with worries, maybe even hopeless in your situation, let me encourage you with the words that Paul writes in Galatians 6:9, "Let us not become weary in doing good, for at the proper time we will reap a harvest if we do not give up." Don't give up, friend. Your breakthrough is right around the bend.

Chapter 8

What's Driving You?

Do not be like the horse or the mule, which have no understanding but must be controlled by bit and bridle or they will not come to you. —Psalm 32:9

Reins are attached to both sides of the bit and are used to tell a horse the direction in which the rider wants it to go. There is an unbelievable variety of bits designed to administer varied amounts of leverage and pressure. Unless you are a professional trainer, you need to do your research to know which bit is best for your horse.

When I first started training Goldie, I used a simple snaffle bit. It is considered to be the "softest" bit with the least amount of pressure; ideal for training young horses. She seemed to do well with that bit for a while. Goldie has always thrived on attention and approval. She has always been a horse eager to please and always loved being doted on. Shortly after she was born, she used to follow me around everywhere I went. We used to play *hide and seek* in the pasture. I would run out into the pasture and lie down in the tall grass, waiting for her to come to find me.

I remember so vividly, one of my fondest memories of our relationship. I was sitting on Danny and Terry's barn floor and Goldie, as a foal, was laying in my lap. I cannot adequately describe the feeling. My dream come true, my very own palomino horse. At this moment in time was a tiny little fuzzy, affectionate, cuddly little foal, who loved my company so much that she was perfectly content lying in my lap soaking up my strokes through her mane. I was in heaven. Until Danny finished sending the other horses out of the barn to the pasture.

"Alright you ugly little rat. It's your turn to go outside." Danny said in his usual playful way to Goldie as he returned to the barn.

"Don't talk to my girl that way!" I said jokingly back to Danny.

"Kid, get that thing off a ya. She ain't no lap dog, ya know. She's a horse." Danny chided me.

"You quit being a bully and leave my girl alone." I joked again.

"Ok, but if you keep that up, one day you're gonna have trouble. It won't be so cute when you got a thousand-pound horse tryin' to sit in your lap." Danny warned me.

Oh, if I had only known how right he was. I loved Goldie so much. I only saw how sweet she was. Truth be told, I struggled with disciplining her because I didn't want to be mean to her. Well, to be honest, I saw her as perfect, never doing anything wrong that would require discipline. I saw her as a friend more than my horse. The affection that we shared was so profound and things were wonderful until it came to training. That's when I realized that I should've listened to Danny.

Training a horse to carry a rider requires the horse to submit to the leadership of the rider. This requires trust and respect in the leadership. How was Goldie going to trust, respect, and submit to me as her leader, when I've taught her all of her life that we're best friends: we're equals?

In the spiritual context, our perception of God affects the way that we relate to him which affects how we respond to being under his training. For some of us, we view him as harsh and angry; always ready to punish severely. With that belief, we can wear ourselves out, always trying to behave perfectly out of fear of punishment or desperately trying to have approval. We may even give up trying to please God and angrily turn away from him. Some people run the risk of viewing themselves and God as buddies and therefore have the belief that God's standards of holy behavior are more of a suggestion than expectation. In those situations, they don't concern themselves with learning how to change sinful behavior because they assume that because of God's love, he doesn't care about behavior. Neither of these beliefs is accurate. We need to try to understand the vastness of God's holiness to have a proper attitude of reverence of him. Additionally, we need to understand that as our Creator, he has authority over everything, including us. However, he loves us so fiercely that, he also desires friendship with us. God is the epitome of love and is also just, so while he may have seeming impossible expectations of us, he exercises his authority with love and patience and discipline appropriate for our level of ability. Not to mention that he gave us his Spirit to help us achieve the expectations that he has for us.

When it came time for training Goldie, she may have been unsure of the process, but her naivety made her compliant and she had a childlike faith in me. Until she realized her autonomy. She realized that really, she doesn't HAVE to do anything if she doesn't want to. This resulted in her challenging my leadership and why wouldn't she? After all, all this time, I showed her that we were equal and were just buddies. Truth be told, it also taught me that I didn't know as much about horse training as I thought I did. She figured that out in a hurry and it damaged her confidence in me and my own confidence in myself and neither of us trusted the other. Our relationship was deteriorating quickly.

Eventually, I took Goldie to a trainer and the trainer suggested that I use a different bit. She had one on hand and let me use it while we were keeping her under training. Honestly, the new bit made a world of difference, but I could tell that Goldie's change was only outward behavioral change. She may have been compliant, but it was forced compliance. She still carried her head high, her muscles were still tense, and even with the new bit, she occasionally protested with dangerous outbursts. The bit persuaded her to pick her reasons for outbursts carefully, but it did absolutely nothing to miraculously restore our trust in one another.

I desperately gobbled up as much information as I could, trying to learn as much as I could. I recognized that I needed to learn how to be the leader that Goldie needed me to be for her to trust me. That is when I set up barrels, poles and obstacles and we spent months just playing around in the yard, but my adventurous heart was yearning for trail riding. I had plenty of friends who had asked me frequently if I wanted to meet for trail riding, but at that time, I'd always been afraid to trailer Goldie by myself (this was before selling Willow to Kelee). I was at a point, where desperation made me take a big gulp, swallow hard, and try and proved to be a game-changer for me.

Soon, I was hauling Goldie to several different places, riding with friends and their horses. Riding with my friends and their horses helped me to feel safe and secure, which in turn, made Goldie safe and secure. Instead of getting on, holding my breath, and feeling tense (which transferred to Goldie), I was able to once again, relax and really enjoy riding (which also transferred to Goldie). Riding with friends helped me to stay calm when Goldie would get spooked, and I was able to assure her and help her stay calm. The more that we rode together, the more that I could read her and the more quickly I could respond to her. I began to see things differently. She's a horse. Horses are prey animals. Horses' natural instincts for self-preservation is to be highly alert to potential danger and then to react and run away from that danger as quickly as possible

For her and I to have a relaxing, fun, safe, trail ride, she needed to trust my judgment of what was dangerous and what wasn't, and she needed to trust that I would get us safely home. As a prey animal, any rustling in the brush could be a predator, requiring her to run away quickly. However, she may not know that the rustling in the brush was only the wind blowing, something that wasn't a threat to her safety. When she was scared, she needed to trust that I would help her work through her fear. Without that trust, she could only depend on her survival instincts to keep her safe and alive.

At that time, my relationship with Goldie was a living metaphor for my relationship with God. My way of life had become one of simple survival. Although I had moments of relaxation and enjoyment, I was always aware and on guard and at the first hint of danger, I was always ready for flight or fight.

I needed to retrain my mind and body to distinguish between real threats and perceived threats. Thankfully as my creator and designer, God is the perfect trainer for me. He knows which bit is best, offering just the right amount of pressure and leverage that's needed for correction.

As I look back on my life, I see my growth as very similar to Goldie's. Before I became a born again Christian, I coped with the pain and sorrow, by chasing any sip of happiness that the world could offer. After I gave my life to Jesus, I followed him wherever he sent me, because, like a child (and Goldie as a foal), I had blind trust in him because of his protection and blessings. I was expecting him to protect and rescue me from every stressful situation. It was relatively easy following him because many of the situations that he was leading me to, I agreed with. I agreed with going to college. and moving to another city a couple of hours away to further my education. Even if it meant struggles, they were struggles that I was familiar with anyway.

Then the life-shattering struggles (ones that I wasn't prepared for) came. I never saw these coming because I believed that Jesus was going to protect me from those kinds of painful struggles. I became like Goldie in our early years when I would try to ride her off our property. While on our property, in her familiar surroundings, with her familiar herd mates nearby, she would ride fine. But as soon as we'd leave the property and start to ride away from the farm, she would stop and plant her feet. She would start backing up quickly, and then she would toss her head and rear. She didn't trust me to take her into the unknown away from her buddies. I can't blame her, I didn't have the skills necessary to prove myself a worthy leader for her.

Like Goldie, my trust in Jesus was shaken. I was faced with the reality that I didn't trust him to take me out to deep waters. I didn't want to be taken out into the deep waters, yet here I was. The trials and sorrows were numerous and came at me like rapid fire. I felt like the Biblical man, Job. I knew the story well. It was one of my favorite stories. God had so much confidence in Job's righteousness that he allowed Satan to afflict Job with different sorrows; but God established the parameters. God was still in control. He only allowed Satan to go so far.

The book of Job also encourages me because Job started off pretty amazing. He lost everything but could say in Job 1:21, "Naked I came from my mother's womb, and naked I will depart. The Lord gave and the Lord has taken away; may the name of the Lord be praised." Even when his wife taunted him and mocked his integrity, he said to her, "You are talking like a foolish woman. Shall we accept good from God and not trouble?" His faith always amazed and encouraged me.

Admittedly, I am amused by the idea that perhaps sometimes my suffering could be happening because God is so confident in my love for him that he allows Satan to afflict me so that I can give him (Satan) a metaphorical black eye. However, something strange happens in Job. His friends come to comfort him. At first things seem to be well. They come and sit with him for seven days, no one saying anything; then things take a turn. Job speaks honestly, out of the deep, overwhelming sorrow of his heart. He says that he wishes he were never born because the sorrow is too great for him to bear. He doesn't understand why these things have happened to him. Remember, he wasn't privy to the challenge between God and Satan in heaven as we are I know that I've experienced wounds of this nature, myself. I have struggled with depression and suicidal ideation for most of my life. Depression gave me a personality that naturally gravitates towards negative perceptions. Sorrows exasperated these thoughts to the point that I've contemplated numerous ways of how I could commit suicide. The thoughts going through my mind during those times ranged from "I can't handle this anymore" to "everyone would be better off without me."

God always intervened by putting images of my children's faces in my mind to help me find myself. Knowing the trauma that they would suffer because of my weakness has been my motivation for pressing on. However, because of the nature of the discussion, it has always been difficult for me to find someone to talk to about these feelings. I really didn't want to end my life, but the pain felt so unbearable. What I really needed was to be able to talk with someone honestly. To say, "This pain hurts so bad that I feel like death is preferable." It's not so much about wanting to die, it's that the pain hurts so bad. In the pain, I truly felt like I absolutely couldn't bear any more. Additionally, depression steals a person's ability to hope. Hope sees the possible and gives a person the motivation to keep going. Without the ability to hope, you don't have a reason to keep going. I truly felt like I couldn't go on. The effort to go on required more strength and courage than I had left within me. I wasn't looking for someone to fix my problems. Many of the problems that I faced couldn't be fixed by anyone, anyways. However, there was always the fear of how people would react to my honesty. I didn't want anyone thinking that I'd "gone off the deep end" and then have me committed. I feared a sterile room with impersonal interrogators more than facing death.

I am thankful for the people in my life who had the God-given gift of true empathy. I have been able to look into their eyes and see that they know…they've been there. Maybe not necessarily themselves, maybe someone that they love has struggled with suicidal ideation, but when looking into their eyes, I have seen authentic emotion. I have felt a connection between our spirits as though there was an invisible cord of shared and understood sorrow joining us.

Unfortunately, when Job bares his heart, instead of listening with compassion, his friends take this opportunity to give him a theological education. What's worse is that their theology states that because he's suffering, obviously he must have sinned pretty badly, and so as awful as it is, he probably deserves it. Of course, they do offer him advice on how to deal with it. He just needs to repent of all the wrong he's done.

Well-meaning people are sometimes guilty of doing this very thing, even today. I can't blame people. Suffering is messy. People have a hard time knowing how to handle their own suffering, let alone knowing how to advise someone else on how to handle theirs; especially when it comes to such serious and disturbing subjects as suicidal thoughts. They want to offer Godly, truth-based advice, but how, especially when the reason for the suffering is unknown? Paul writes in 1 Corinthians 13:1, "If I speak in the tongues of men or of angels, but do not have love, I am only a resounding gong or a clanging cymbal." If we have wisdom and discernment to understand God's word correctly, but we don't have love, we are loud and obnoxious and even painful to the ears.

What I've learned through my suffering, is that what I need more than sound doctrine or advice, is someone to just sit and hurt with me. To help me feel that I'm not going to have to endure this alone and that I'm free to express the agony in my heart openly and honestly without judgement or condemnation. Interestingly, David knew that God could handle his raw honesty when he wrote his psalms, yet for some reason, some people today feel that they have to correct another person's expressions of their sorrow to protect God's dignity?

In my early faith years, in my own deep suffering, I became rebellious of God's leadership, not because I was being willfully obstinate, but because I was terrified. I screamed, I cried, I pounded my fists on the floor. "Why God? Why would you allow this to happen to me?" "Haven't I faithfully followed you? Why didn't you protect me? Why aren't you protecting my children? Don't you love me anymore? Or maybe you don't love me that much?" I knew in my heart that none of that was true. I knew that God loved me fiercely, he proved it by sending Jesus to die for my sins on the cross. Logically, I knew that my suffering was not God's fault, it was a result of human free will. Then I wrestled with thoughts like, "Am I being punished for the sins of my past?" "Am I cursed? Is my family cursed?" I couldn't make sense of anything and I couldn't shake the fear that shrouded me. God chose not to intervene; he chose not to protect me from this pain and suffering. If God wasn't going to protect me, where in this awful world would I be safe? What did this mean for me as a Christian? What did this mean regarding my faith in God?

Exhausted from the sobbing and pounding of my fists, I collapsed onto the floor and I whispered to God, "God, I'm not walking away from you, but I have no strength to walk with you. I don't want to be disobedient, but I'm paralyzed by my fear. I don't want to take another step. If you want me to go somewhere with you, you're gonna have to carry me. I don't know what else to do." I felt a supernatural peace come over me. Like all the yuck inside of me was released and a huge weight was lifted from my chest. I heard God whisper to me, "I know. I know how much you hurt. But I promise you, child. I will never ask you to give anyone more grace than you've been given. And I will help you. I know you're tired. I know you're weak. I will carry you."

I believe that this was a necessary experience for showing me the truth about my relationship with God. Was I really obeying God all this time? Or was I going along with him because his plan was in agreement with my plan?

Day by day, I got up and did my everyday life. It was living day by day. That was all that I had strength for. I had no strength for hope. I was doing the bare necessities to get through each day, but over time, I felt the wounds healing. Every day I simply relied on God's love. It was strange to me at the time. I felt like I was letting God down like I should be doing something to please him. I should be working and proving to him how much I love him, but I had no energy, no desire to do anything. I felt dead inside, barely hanging on. I needed to cling to him and rely on his love for me to be able to make it through each day. Over time, I grew to understand and appreciate the fact that this is all God really wants from me. Sometimes, simple surrender is the deepest form of obedience that we can muster up. Relying on him every step of the way is all we can do.

For several more years, more devastation occurred in my life. Many times, I would just lie on my bathroom floor in a fetal position and just let God's love wash over me. I needed to just bask in his love.

I experienced an anxiety attack while driving and it was so bad that I couldn't continue driving and had to be taken to the emergency room. I also began having anxiety attacks nearly every night. I would wake up out of a deep sleep, sweating, gripped with fear, hyperventilating and sobbing. There was no specific incident that served as a trigger. The only thing that would calm me was having Tony pray over me. Peace would cover me and I would fall back asleep as quickly as I had been awakened.

As I look back on it, I realize that although I continued to love God, I had developed a fear of His will. I stopped asking him for things or help because I was afraid. I remained close to him and continued to thank and praise him for his continual mercies, but I just stopped asking for his protection. I knew enough to know that God didn't orchestrate the suffering in my life, and I knew that it wasn't that he COULDN'T protect me. It was that he chose not to protect me.

I knew from Romans 8:28 that God works all things for the good of those who love him, but the things that had been thrown at me were heavy, heavy stuff, in rapid succession. I became neurotic and hyper-vigilant over my family. I was like a mother hen chasing her chicks, trying to keep them under her wings. "No, no! Don't go there!" "No, no, come back here." "No, no, don't do that." "If you do what I say, just as I say, then I can keep you safe."

The more things that happened, the harder I tried to keep everything together. The harder I tried to keep things together, the more things fell apart. I saw my family -everything that I held dear- crumbling through my fingers like sand. I guess I was terrified of God's will for my life because it became evident that suffering was included. I couldn't see how any good come out of all this suffering and quite honestly, I didn't care about what good would come out of it. It was too costly for me. But trying to control everything and everyone wasn't working. My marriage was falling apart, my children all left home. My two oldest sons graduated from high school and moved out. Tim started college and Daniel joined the National Guard. My two youngest children, Dylan and Jen, went to live with their father. This devastated me because I knew the environment that they'd be living in and I'd have even less control to protect them. I was a wreck.

Then something remarkable happened. It was close to Easter and I went to a Christian conference. Although I continued to stay near to Jesus, I had stopped going to church. While at this conference, I closed my eyes and saw an altar in my mind. I knew in my spirit that God was wanting me to surrender my children over to him. I remember thinking in my mind, *No, God, please don't ask me to do that. I'm not ready to take my hands off them, yet.*

God whispered to me, "This is the only way for you to have peace. I love you and I love your children even more than you do, but the only way that you're going to have peace is if you trust me with them."

I wrestled in my mind, my soul was in such agony, but then I took a deep breath and said, "Ok, God, if this is the only way, I trust you." In my mind, I "walked" each one of my children up to the altar and told God that I was giving each of them to him. I was releasing my control over them to him. An inexplicable peace washed over me and tears flowed down my cheeks. I felt a sense of relief that I hadn't felt in a long time.

A few months later, my daughter was in a car accident. I went to the hospital and arrived after the doctors were moving her on a stretcher. She was unconscious and had a neck brace on. My heart was broken and I was physically sick. The doctors assured me that the neck brace was only standard procedure until she regained consciousness. They stated that as far as they could tell, she had no injuries other than a scrape on her forehead. I thanked God.

It was several weeks later that I went with her to look at her car. Again, I was physically sick. The car was so damaged, that the first thought that came to mind was that by all rights, she should have been dead. I knew in my spirit that God was showing me this to let me know that I really can trust him with my children. Although he allowed the accident, he sent his angels to protect her life.

For the next couple of years, my children continued to experience trials and situations that should've gone wrong for them, but miraculously, they always seemed to come out of it alive. The evidence of God's protection over them cannot be denied. I still struggle with a tendency to worry. I don't know if I'll ever get to the point of "no-worry" this side of eternity. However, at least my worry doesn't cripple me like it used to.

Courage is being scared to death, but saddling up anyway. —John Wayne

The story of Job is such a fascinating book about suffering and how God responds to human suffering. God does intervene with Job's complaints by making it clear to him that God is God and Job is a mere man. Job does not have the abilities, the knowledge or the wisdom to advise God on how to do his job. However, he also confronted Job's friends and told them that they were wrong in how they handled Job's suffering and that he would have Job pray for them. He also restored to Job more than he had lost before.

The book of Job taught me so many things. First, it taught me that there is a spiritual battle going on, which we humans are in the middle of. There are things going on that we don't see or understand, so we need to be humble when trying to help others. Secondly, it taught me that God can handle my honest expression of my pain and sorrow. Thirdly, it taught me that God is infinitely wiser and more capable than me and that I can trust him. Fourth, it taught me that God will not only bring good out of my suffering, but the good that he brings is vastly better than anything that I could imagine. He not only restored all of my relationships, but he's made the love between us stronger than I ever thought it could be!

Over the years, God has revealed several prophecies to me that have come true exactly as he foretold. These things have strengthened my faith that God is with me and my family. He is trustworthy and he'll carry me when I am too weak to walk on my own, helping me to challenge my anxiety.

This lesson became very vivid to me one-day several years later. Goldie and I were on a trail ride near our home. The relationship between Goldie and I had grown to where this day we had left the farm on our own. Can you believe it? We had grown in our trust in one another that we were riding off together, without relying on the skills and confidence of other horses and riders!

We were walking down the minimum maintenance road and I was riding her bareback and bitless with just a rope halter and reins attached to the halter. As we were riding along, completely relaxed, I marveled at how far we had come. I marveled at how our relationship had grown to where I could move her in the direction I wanted to go with only a nudge of my feet. Our relationship had grown to where I could feel what she was feeling through her body, and I could reassure her more quickly. I like the idea that I don't have to have a saddle on or a bit in her mouth because I want trail riding to be as comfortable and pleasant for her as possible. I want her to look forward to and enjoy trail riding with me. I want her to enjoy fellowship with me as much as I enjoy it with her.

That's when it dawned on me, that perhaps, this is exactly what God wants with each of us. This life is like a long, adventurous trail ride. There are gonna be obstacles. Maybe mud bogs to struggle through, steep hills with rocky terrain to cover, narrow paths with trees growing tightly together and difficult to navigate through, mountains to climb, or real danger like a bear encounter, or just a deer that jumps out and startles us; or maybe it's nothing, but just the wind rustling the brush. But God wants us to trust him to get us through it. He knows things that we don't and the more that we trust him, the less that we need to panic and act in a way that requires correction from harsh bits; the less that we try to buck him off creates no need for a saddle, which makes a more pleasurable ride for us. And to think that that's what God wants, too. He actually wants so badly to enjoy this ride with us, that he encourages a relationship between us so close-- that we are so in tune to his leading that we will go with just the nudging of the Spirit, that way the ride will be easy, fun, and enjoyable for us. He actually delights in sharing the ride with us. He and us, embarking on an adventure together!

Chapter 9

Leading the Way

In your unfailing love you will lead the people you have redeemed. In your strength you will guide them to your holy dwelling. **—Exodus 15:13**

Very few activities with my horses have tried my patience like loading into the trailer. There is nothing worse than getting excited about going someplace to find out that your horse disagrees with you and wishes to stay home. Well, there is one thing worse, and that is NEEDING to get someplace in a hurry and your horse refuses to load. Thankfully, I've never been in that situation.

There is no place for pride when dealing with horses, because they find a way of humbling you, or in unfortunate circumstances, humiliating you. One such situation occurred at the Pillsbury State Forest. Tony and I loaded Goldie and Blaze and were looking forward to a day trip of riding in the state forest. However, once we got the horses unloaded and tied to a high line, and we were unloading our gear, we discovered that I'd forgotten Goldie's bridle. Granted, we weren't far from home, but far enough that it didn't make any sense to go back home just to get a bridle. Disappointed, we decided that we might as well just reload the horses and return home.

We have a four-horse stock trailer, however, I learned in a quick hurry that it is not wise to tie both Goldie and Blaze together upfront. That being said, the dividing gate that separates the front half from the back half, is set so that the distance for the front half is greater than that of the back half. Blaze is bigger and longer than Goldie, so he has to go in first. Thankfully, Goldie is a compact model and fits perfectly in the back half.

We started to load Blaze but he refused to load. We tried walking him in circles, we tried backing him over long distances, we tried lunging him, we even tried using the lunge line as a butt strap, we tried weaving the lunge line through the trailer and out one of the windows and "winching" him into the trailer. Onlookers advised us to use a whip just to tap him and let him know that we mean business. That was a big mistake. As soon as he saw the whip in my hand, he whipped his butt around in my direction, backed towards me and gave out a warning kick.

It was downright humiliating and we all were starting to get hot. I was feeling bad for Goldie because she had been standing tied this whole time and hadn't had any water. We decided that Tony should just take Goldie home and then come back to get Blaze and I.

After Tony returned, we tried loading Blaze again, still with no luck. The next thing we knew, a very big man came over to help. He got right behind Blaze and pushed him into the trailer! I think the only reason why it worked was that Blaze was too bewildered to resist. I decided right then and there that we needed to spend a few weeks schooling in trailer loading.

I've learned from Blaze, that he is very sensitive to the emotions of his handlers. As soon as he detects frustration, his energy increases. I don't think he's an anxious horse whose anxiety escalates around anxious energy. He comes off to me as a proud horse, almost like he's insulted that anyone would dare talk to or treat him in such a manner. At any rate, maintaining as neutral emotion as possible has had the best results with him.

In working on loading, this was crucial. At any moment when he felt like I was pressuring him too much or too quickly, he would snap his head back and rear. I got nowhere…fast. I found that what worked best for him was to maintain consistent light, pressure, and then release the pressure and gush about how proud I was of him at the slightest try. Step by step, we did this until he was standing at the front of the trailer, eating the grain from the manger. Like the old saying, "inch by inch, life's a cinch."

I believe that sometimes God works with me this way. He understands my anxious personality. He knows how difficult new experiences are for me. Yet, he also knows how important these experiences are for my growth. So, he allows some pressure that's just uncomfortable enough to make me step forward, then he lets me pause as he lavishes praise onto me, before applying more pressure to make me take the next step. Conversely, he allows the pressure to remain for as long as I refuse to submit and move forward. I'd love to say that we cured his loading woes, but that wouldn't be true. Blaze has his good days and his bad. Most of the time, he loads right up when we're leaving our place. Returning home, is when we have the most difficulty loading him. Looking at myself, I'm a lot like this. I have my good days and I have my bad days. Some days I find that I follow God relatively easily, almost like dancing. Other days, I imagine I'm a lot like Blaze, planting my feet into the ground and leaning all of my weight against God's lead rope.

Paul writes about this paradox in Romans 7:15-24. In a nutshell, Paul talks about the spiritual war going on inside of himself, between the Holy Spirit and his sinful nature. He wants to do good, but he can't. He doesn't want to sin, but he can't help it. He agrees that the expectations of God are good, but he can't fulfill them. Praise be to God for his grace!

The trials that God has taken me through had made me feel as claustrophobic as Blaze might when stepping onto the trailer. There have been rough patches in my life that have rattled me and scared me with uncertainty, similarly to how Blaze might feel riding along gravel roads in the trailer.

The thing I found to be absolutely crucial in my leadership roles as mother of my children and manager of staff, is that the people that you're leading will be more willing to obey your directions if they trust and respect you. It is a humbling experience to have the voluntary submission and obedience of a 1200–1400-pound animal who retains a mind, will and instincts of its own. At any time, this amazing animal could exercise her power to throw me off of her back, causing me devastating injury. At any moment this animal could charge me, bite me or kick me, again, causing devastating injury. While distributing hay out in the pasture, all 4 horses come running, excited for the hay, jockeying with one another for first dibs. At any moment, any one of them could trample me; but they don't. They choose to be careful. They choose to be conscious of my space. They choose to surrender their power to do what they want, to pursue their own desires, to preserve their own safety, in deference and trust in my leadership and authority over them. That, my friend, is humbling.

In my opinion, any being that is conscious of its own free will, yet chooses to lay down that free will in submission to another -even allowing that other being to exercise their own free will over them-, is not displaying weakness, but rather trust, strength and courage. It isn't a hard thing to use one's power to influence, intimidate or bully others into getting what one wants. It takes tremendous courage to refrain from using that power and instead, submitting and trusting in the power of the authority over them.

An important part of building trust and respect is being patient and compassionate. It is like the old saying (that applies to people and horses) "no one cares about how much you know until they know how much you care." Jesus is the greatest model of this. Philippians 2:5-7 says, "In your relationships with one another, have the same mindset as Christ Jesus: who being in the very nature God, did not consider equality with God something to be used to his own advantage; rather, he made himself nothing by taking the very nature of a servant, being made in human likeness."

Isn't it interesting that Jesus demonstrated to us that being a good leader starts with becoming a good servant? Imagine this for a minute. Jesus (as the Word of God) created everything (See John 1:1-4). Yet he came to earth in the form of a human baby in order to relate to us as fellow humans. He is more than competent in leading us. He is not a harsh, demanding leader. He knows our limitations and our weaknesses and he is patient and compassionate with us. Additionally, many years ago, I discovered a profound truth in Jesus' example in John 13:5 tells us, "The evening meal was in progress, and the devil had already prompted Judas, the son of Simon Iscariot, to betray Jesus. Jesus knew that the Father had put all things under his power and that he had come from God and was returning to God, so he got up from the meal, took off his outer clothing, and wrapped a towel around his waist. After that, he poured water into a basin and began to wash his disciples' feet, drying them with the towel that was wrapped around him." Jesus (God in flesh) took on the role of a servant, and not just any servant, but probably one of the least respected servants in that culture. Those servants were the ones whose jobs were washing the feet of guests. Jesus even washed the feet of the two men who he knew would cause him great sorrow--Judas through his betrayal, and Peter through his denial. How was he able to do this? I believe the answer lies in verse 3. Because Jesus knew who he was and where he was going, he was able to act in humble strength. He wasn't afraid of what people thought of him, performing a servant's job. He wasn't afraid that he would look weak or like a sissy. He wasn't concerned with protecting his heart by skipping over the two people that he knew would break his heart. Why? Because his confidence was in who he was and where he was going. As believers, we have the same ability if we keep our focus on who we are in Christ, and where we're going.

We all find ourselves in dual positions. We are leaders over some while following others that are charged with leading us. Peter gives us instruction in 1 Peter 2:13-25 that those of us who are believers are expected to submit to all authority regardless of whether they are considerate or harsh. The expectation of our submission to authority is not based on the qualifications of the person in authority, it is based on the command of God, himself. Whether the leader conducts himself/herself in a manner that is worthy of submission is irrelevant. Yes, it makes it easier for us to submit, but God expects us to submit to the authority whether we feel like it or not. I do believe that in certain circumstances, it is appropriate and even necessary to disobey authority. In the case of an abusive marriage, it may be necessary to leave the marriage if you or your children's safety is at risk[1]. Additionally, resisting authority may be appropriate if a person/entity with authority over you expects you to violate a command of God. As Peter states in Acts 5:29, "We must obey God rather than human beings."

I'm not here to tell anyone what this is supposed to look like in your life and your family. I'm a firm believer that each person needs to go to God and get direction from him directly on all matters. He knows you and your family best, and he knows how to guide and direct best.

---

[1] If you are in this situation please pray for God's direction and seek people who will join you in prayer. Even though you may have to leave your home for your safety, you may not have to end your marriage. God still performs miracles today and can heal the brokenness in your spouse, and restore your marriage and your family.

Paul writes in Ephesians 6:9, "And masters (in today's context we could consider it as an instruction to employers), treat your slaves (and similarly, employees) in the same way. Do not threaten them, since you know that he who is both their Master and yours is in heaven, and there is no favoritism with him." Additionally, Colossians 4:1 says, "Masters (employers) provide your slaves (employees) with what is right and fair, because you know that you also have a Master in heaven." Employers are expected to treat their employees with gentleness and fairness because that is how God, as our Master, treats us. Although Jesus did not challenge the practice of slavery directly, he was very explicit in commanding us to love God and love other people. In following those two commands, slavery and other social issues would virtually disappear. Jesus came to abolish "rule-keeping" and instead came to transform hearts. He understood that laws and rules may affect external change, but rarely does that produce genuine change in attitudes. Our attitudes towards people are what motivates our behaviors towards people. Genuine attitude change can only be accomplished by heart trans-formation. That is what Jesus came to offer.

The Apostle Paul, having received direct revelation from Jesus, challenged the ways that slave owners and slaves related to one another, and thereby provided a revolutionary change of mindset regarding the practice. Paul writes to believers in Galatians 3:26-29, "So in Christ Jesus, you are all chil-dren of God through faith, for all of you who were baptized into Christ have clothed yourselves with Christ. There is neither Jew nor Gentile, neither slave nor free, nor is there male and female, for you are all one in Christ Jesus. If you belong to Christ, then you are Abraham's seed, and heirs according to the promise." What Paul is saying here is that there should be such a spirit of unity between believers that we aren't prejudiced by the differences in race, social class, or gender; we should see ourselves as equals -joint heirs in Christ-. Having that perspective changes the way that we treat others. Addi-tionally, in Romans 13:10, he writes, "Love does no harm to a neighbor. Therefore, love is the fulfillment of the law." Paul gives a practical application of this in the story of Onesimus, a slave that ran away from his master to Paul, and Paul's letter to Onesimus' master, Philemon.

There are many difficult scenarios in the Bible, however, it is important to remember the culture and the context in which it was written. We need the Spirit's help in discerning how to understand the historical context of its time, while at the same time gleaning principles that can be applied to us for today.

Getting back to our discussion regarding employers and employees, if you are asking employees to do something beyond their current capabilities, they need to know that you will help them and give them the tools that they need to do what you're asking them to do -and equally important- that you won't harshly punish them while they're learning. They need to know that you genuinely care about them as individuals. You must have the capabilities and competency as a leader but it absolutely must be balanced with humility, compassion and patience.

A mistake that I made with Goldie when she was young and similarly with my children, was that I failed to establish myself as the final authority. In my relationship with Goldie, we were equals. As a single mom, I raised the kids in a manner that looked more like a team. The kids may not have seen us truly as "equals" per se, but in my naivety, I allowed them to believe that all things were negotiable. This didn't become a problem until they were old enough to learn that mom doesn't always know everything and they discovered their autonomy. I taught them to think critically and logically, and eventually, they were able to make very sound, valid arguments to support their positions. Because of the "team" style of my parenting, I found myself boxed into corners against their intellect, and in some cases had to take out the "because I'm mom" card. As you can imagine, at times, this did not go over well. It created way more power struggles as we all adjusted to me trying to claim my place of final authority after years of being "just another team player".

It was after marrying Tony, that I learned why God developed the nuclear family as well as the Church family, to have a sensible hierarchy of authority. With Jesus as the head of the whole family, all decisions by each member of the family are made by his authority. His criteria for obedience is "love God above everything, and love others as you love yourself". If every member of the family weighed all of their decisions within the framework of "is this action showing that I love God in all ways" and/or "is this action showing that I love my spouse, children, parents, siblings, neighbors, etc as I love myself", there would be more peace within the family, the Church family and the world.

I have the right to do anything," you say—but not everything is beneficial. "I have the right to do anything"—but not everything is constructive. No one should seek their own good, but the good of others..." —1 Corinthians 10:23-24

Do not cause anyone to stumble, whether Jews, Greeks or the Church of God. —Verse 32

Paul tells us what that looks like within the nuclear family in Ephesians 5:21-26. "Submit to one another out of reverence for Christ. Wives, submit yourselves to your own husbands as you do to the Lord. For the husband is the head of the wife as Christ is the head of the church, his body, of which he is the Savior. Now as the church submits to Christ, so also wives should submit to their husbands in everything. Husbands, love your wives, just as Christ loved the church and gave himself up for her to make her holy, cleansing her by the washing with water through the word, and to present her to himself as a radiant church, without stain or wrinkle or any other blemish, but holy and blameless. In the same way, husbands ought to love their wives as their own bodies." Paul is calling husbands to love their wives by willfully laying down their rights to their wants and needs in favor of meeting their wives' wants/needs, just as Jesus sacrificed himself for the church.

Peter also addresses husbands in 1 Peter 3:7. In fact, Peter goes further to say that a husband is in danger of his prayers being left unheard if he fails to love his wife and treat her with respect. Peter includes an instruction to wives in 1 Peter 3:1. Paul continues in Ephesians 6:1-4 "Children, obey your parents in the Lord, for this is right. 'Honor your father and mother' which is the first commandment with a promise--that it may go well with you and that you may enjoy long life on the earth. Fathers do not exasperate your children; instead, bring them up in the training and instruction of the Lord."

In Genesis 1:26-27 "Then God said, 'Let us make man in our image, in our likeness, so that they may rule over the fish in the sea and the birds in the sky, over the livestock and all the wild animals and over all the creatures that move along the ground.' So, God created man in his own image, in the image of God he created them; male and female he created them." So, the first thing we notice here, is God is speaking of himself as in the plural: "Let us make man in OUR image, in OUR likeness." This is evidence of God's triune nature -the Trinity-. The Bible tells us in John 4:24 that God is Spirit. Apart from coming to earth in the form of Jesus, God has no physical form. So, I think it's safe to say that when God created "man" in his image and likeness, he was speaking of creating human beings with his attributes. God, without physical form, has both masculine and feminine attributes that he imparted to physical beings, humans. Thus, the creation of men and women. Just as each person within the Trinity has a distinct role, so men and women were created to have distinct roles. Each person within the Trinity, functioning in his specific roles, makes up a complete wholeness of God. Similarly, as husbands and wives' function within their specific roles, it makes up a complete wholeness of the nuclear family.

God created the husband uniquely as the primary provider and protector of the household and worthy of the respect due to such a challenging position. God has placed the primary responsibility of the entire wellbeing; spiritually, financially, emotionally, and physically, upon the husband. That is a tremendous amount of responsibility. God created woman as a help-mate for the man. She supplements where he is lacking. Many people misunderstand this to mean that the wife is inferior to her husband. They read it as she is "just" her husband's helper. That is not how God intended it. If you remember back in Genesis 2 when God created man, he saw that it was not good that the man was alone. So, God decided to make a helper suitable for him. God made all of the animals and brought them to the man, but no suitable helper was found. So that's when God created woman.

Notice that the man and all of the animals were made from dirt, but not the woman. The woman was the only creation that was not made from dirt. She came from the man's rib. As a fellow human from human flesh, she is equal to man, however, the role that she fills as a wife, is subordinate in the family to the husband. The wife complements the husband with her gifts that he is lacking and vice versa. In that sense, they are partners, however, when a decision has to be made where they can't agree, she is called to submit to the final authority of her husband.

Think of it like a business or corporation. There is a hierarchy of authority from the president or CEO down to the janitor. It doesn't mean that the people in those positions are greater than or less than in value to one another, it just means that the positions that they fill are greater than or less than in responsibility and authority of one another. A hierarchy of authority is necessary because if everyone had final authority, how would a decision be made? If no one had final authority, how would decisions be made? There has to be a chain of command.

God created the woman as a "suitable" helper to man. To help him make decisions. She helps balance or complement him. She brings a perspective that he may not have considered. So, with the two strengths combined, it gives the family a greater chance for success. The children, are to submit to the authority of their parents, however, as the Scriptures say, fathers are to exercise their authority over their children in a way that draws them closer to God, not in a way that is harsh and pushes them away.

The key is in exercising the authority in humility, love and sacrifice over the ones that you are head of. This can be followed down the leadership of the wives to the children. I believe that this is the best model for any leadership position. Paul writes in Romans 12:3, "For by the grace given me I say to every one of you: Do not think of yourself more highly than you ought, but rather think of yourself with sober judgment, in accordance with the faith God has distributed to each of you." I believe what Paul is writing here, is that we are to be willing to see ourselves as God sees us, with strengths but also with limitations and opportunities for personal growth, ourselves. We have to have a healthy, whole view of ourselves.

Having experienced domestic violence, I understand the aversion that some women may have to submitting to the authority of their husbands. It took me a long time of working with God to heal from my past in order to be able to hear these Scriptures without feeling angry with God for creating this hierarchy. I realized that abusive husbands weren't in God's plan in the hierarchy. Again, husbands are called to love their wives as Jesus loved the Church--even dying for her.

God also showed me my own parts of the problems in my first marriage. Had I been a born again Christian and was able to follow the teaching in 1 Peter 3:1-6 of being a wife with a quiet, humble spirit, things could've been very different. I was more like the quarrelsome wife described in Proverbs 21, 25, and 27. I really struggled with anger, guilt and shame for many years after my divorce, but God spoke to me and told me that in order to experience peace, I had to repent of my sins in our marriage. The world fed my pride with justifications and excuses, but true to his word, God's peace covered me once I confessed my sins that contributed to the breakdown and asked God for his forgiveness. Speaking it out loud, honestly and without justifications, asking for forgiveness and experiencing his love and forgiveness, helped heal my heart and gave me peace.

Being a single mom was tough. Every problem of raising and maintaining a household was mine and mine alone. It was my responsibility to figure out how the bills were going to be paid. It was my responsibility to make sure the kids were growing and developing into what would be responsible, moral adults. It was my responsibility to keep the car running. A flat tire in the middle of nowhere with no cell phone reception and a carload of little children depending on you to get them home? Guess I'm getting out the jack, 4-way wrench and the spare and learning how to change a tire. God did not design the woman to carry such responsibilities alone. Can it be done? Yes, many women are proof of what can be done when it needs to be done. However, if we're honest with ourselves, it's hard and it hardens our hearts. In order to handle all of these burdens, we develop a toughness necessary for survival and we risk losing our softness, our gentleness, and our nurturing instincts. This is not how God designed it to be.

The family is a beautiful balance of mutual love, respect, discipline, authority, and submission when done God's way.

Chapter 10

Knowledge and Wisdom: Where do yours Come from?

If any of you lacks wisdom, you should ask God, who gives generously to all without finding fault, and it will be given to you.
—James 1:5

In the business of horse training, there are as many different theories and techniques as there are horses. For an average horse owner desiring to train their own horse, this variety of perspectives can be helpful or it can be a hindrance. I've discovered that it's a lot like raising children. There are so many professionals promoting their particular theories or approaches, and each of them claims to be the right way. Any other approach could have devastating long term results, so they claim.

Now, truth be told, there are certainly wrong ways of handling children or horses. Abuse is wrong, and neglect is wrong. But I think that we've flooded our society with so many so-called experts who are quick to criticize any action that isn't of their particular trademark actions, that we've created parents and horse owners who are confused and lacking confidence in their own instincts. At least that's how I frequently felt both as a mother and a horse owner.

As a novice trainer for my own horses, I found that all the knowledge in the world was useless without wisdom. The wealth of knowledge available to me was astounding. I love that there are so many philosophies and techniques to choose from because each horse is an individual and not every technique will work with every horse. However, learning how to apply what technique and how long to use a particular technique before switching to a different one was frustrating. Wisdom allowed me to interpret how to apply the knowledge to my horses. Wisdom is a gift from God. Remember in Genesis, God gave humans authority over the animals. Therefore, I believe that God gives us wisdom in knowing how to relate to and train those animals. Similarly, God created families in a hierarchy with parents having authority over their children. Therefore, certainly God will give us wisdom in knowing how to raise our children.

Proverbs 2:6 states, "For the Lord gives wisdom, and from his mouth come knowledge and understanding." Hosea 4:6 goes so far as to state, "My people are destroyed for lack of knowledge." More specifically, God is speaking to and through Hosea stating that his people are destroyed for rejecting the knowledge that comes from God, himself. The knowledge of God, about God, and from God.

In today's age of internet and technology, we have an overabundance of information literally at our fingertips. Absorbing that information gives us knowledge, but is all that knowledge truly beneficial to us? I think it's safe to say that there is a lot of knowledge that is not only virtually useless but also harmful.

> *Blessed is the man who does not walk in the counsel of the wicked or stand in the way of the sinners or sit in the seat of mockers. But his delight is in the law of the Lord, and on his law he meditates day and night. He is like a tree planted by streams of water, which yields fruit in season and whose leaf does not wither. Whatever he does prospers.* —Psalm 1:1-3

We've got to learn how to analyze the knowledge of the world, weigh it against the truths in the Bible, ask God for wisdom and discernment in applying the knowledge, but then we also need to rest in the confidence that God's wisdom is enough. We don't have to make ourselves neurotic when things aren't going well. We don't have to listen to the judgment and criticism of those around us.

One of the things that I believe every horse trainer agrees on is that horses need strong leadership. In a herd, every member has a function. The way it has been described to me is that the lead stallion is the protector from danger. The lead mare leads the herd away from the danger to a safe place. The safety of the herd depends on every other member of the herd submitting to the authority of those two leaders. Frequently young stallions will challenge the older lead stallion. A battle takes place and the strongest of them becomes the lead stallion. This is necessary for the survival of the herd. Again, if a member of the herd decides that she doesn't like the lead mare's bossiness and instead chooses to ignore her to continue eating the lush green grass, she could very easily be killed or wounded. Her security comes from being in the herd, trusting the leadership of the lead stallion and mare and acting on that trust in submission and obedience.

The most profound way that I've learned about leadership came through Blaze. It wasn't long after we'd bought Blaze that I noticed that I was increasingly becoming intimidated by him. To be honest, at times, when I asked him to do something that he didn't want to do, he was downright dangerous. I would ask him to lunge and he would rear up and strike at me. Several times, his front hooves would come very close to striking my forearms. I would ask him to load into the trailer and he would quickly turn his body and kick at me. The more and more that I worked with him, the more and more intimidated by him I became. I was doing a lot of research from a lot of different horse trainers, and many of them stated that when a horse is misbehaving, you get them into the round pen and you make them work. The mantra was, "make the wrong thing hard and the right thing easy" and the philosophy was basically, "He who makes the feet move, is the boss." The premise was that when they refused to do what you ask them to do, you move their feet. This philosophy comes from watching herds.

The leader establishes his or her leadership by being the one moving the feet of every other member of the herd. When the leader is hungry and approaches food, everyone else is supposed to move out of the way. If someone doesn't move, the leader says "move" in a "louder tone", by maybe pinning his ears back. If the other still doesn't move. The leader turns up the tone, by maybe stretching his neck out towards the other. If that doesn't get their attention, they might find the leader's teeth in its rump. You get the idea. The leader moves everyone else. As soon as they do what you want them to do, you stop and let them rest. Resting is their reward and it's the way that you communicate to them that they did something right.

Well, I put Blaze in the round pen and asked him to go right. He began walking. Good. I asked him to go into a trot. He began trotting. Good. "Oh, wait! I didn't ask you to change directions!" I tried to cut him off and turn him around. He reared and struck out at me. I knew from my research that I couldn't back down, because then I'm showing submission to him, but I was afraid. My fear quickly became anger (a conditioned response from my history). "NO!" I shouted at him. I cracked the whip at my side onto the ground as hard as I could. I glared at him, pointing to the right, indicating that I wanted him to move right. He reared again and spun his butt towards me and kicked out at me. I smacked the whip against his butt, fear and anger welling up inside of me. "I'm supposed to be the leader here! He's supposed to respect me!" I thought in my head. "MOVE! If you're gonna be a jerk, then I'm gonna make you move!" I yelled at him, pointing to the right with my right hand, whip raised in my left hand. He snorted and ran to the right. Again, he cut across the middle of the pen, seeming to charge at me, but then veering off to the left. "I've been nothing but nice to him. I've treated him well and fairly. Just as I do to Goldie. He's not a horse, he's just an ass!" We stood there breathless, both of us staring each other down. I put him away for the day and went into the house and prayed to God. "God, what am I doing wrong? I'm following everything that these trainers are telling me to do, but it's not working. In fact, things are getting worse. I can't work with this horse! I don't know why you would tell Ellen that we're supposed to have him. He's not a good fit for us. He and I don't get along."

God whispered to my spirit, "The approach isn't wrong, the spirit in which you're doing it is wrong. Try being patient, calm, and understanding when you correct him. The goal is 'correction' not punishment."

The next day I got him in the round pen again and I could tell right away that he was ready for another standoff. I held the whip up in my left hand and pointed with my right hand indicating to him that I wanted him to go right. "Walk." I said, low and softly.

He started walking. I clucked to him, indicating to him that I wanted him to trot. He started trotting, but then immediately spun around into the center of the pen and cut across me. I remembered what God had told me the day before, and took a deep breath.

"Okay, buddy. If that's what you're going to choose, that's fine. That's your choice, but then I'm going to have to make you work." I said it very matter of factly.

I concentrated very hard on keeping as neutral emotion as possible and stepped towards him to cut him off. To my surprise, he moved away from me and began going towards the right! I was in awe! That is when the light bulb came on. He was feeling my angry energy. My angry energy increased his energy. We were feeding off of each other's energy. When I kept my energy calm, then he was calm. It was a great day in the round pen. Later that evening, when I was praying to God, he spoke to me and said, "Blaze is just a horse. He's just doing what a horse does. You can't take it personally, and it doesn't make any sense, nor does it do any good to get mad at him. He is who he is. Respect isn't earned by demanding it. It isn't earned through anger. It is earned through establishing boundaries, and defending those boundaries when they're crossed, with calm, patient, understanding energy."

God went on to show me how Blaze and I got to this point, to begin with. I was relating to Blaze in the same way that I related to Goldie. I didn't appreciate that Blaze is a completely different horse than Goldie. For starters, he's a male and Goldie's a female. That in itself presents major differences in relating. Additionally, they each have very different personalities. We have to also consider history. I've owned Goldie literally all of her life. Ellen had owned Blaze literally all of his life until she sold him to me at 8 years old. Therefore, the relationship that I have with Goldie was vastly different than the relationship (or lack of relationship) that I had with Blaze. I hadn't considered the adjustment that Blaze needed to make in leaving the one friend that he'd had all of his life up to that point. He was as bonded to Ellen as I was to Goldie. He was her number 1. Since Goldie was my best girl -my number 1-, he was relegated to number 2 in my heart.

However, as is my nature with nearly all animals, I had been so quick to welcome Blaze into loving relationship, that I didn't take the time to establish proper boundaries with him. I doted on him, and babied him, and looking back on it, I let him get away with subtle steps of disrespect. Things like pushing into my space whenever he wanted something, bumping me when he was walking with me, allowing him to set the pace of our walking. I was letting him become the leader over me without even realizing it until it had escalated. He wasn't being disobedient. He was confused. He was communicating leadership in horse language, and I didn't see it until it got to the point that when I wanted to be the leader, he was confused because up to that point, he thought he was the leader.

Now that Blaze and I understand one another, we have learned how to respect one another, and I can honestly say, that I love him. He truly is an amazing horse. He is brave, and calm, easy-going, he gives with all of his heart, and he takes care of his rider. All that he asks in return, is that you respect him. I truly am indebted to him for all that he's taught me and built-in my character.

Learning from Blaze showed me how my insecurities about my own self-worth, caused me to fail in setting boundaries when dealing with people. From smaller infractions like peer pressure to avoid being bullied, to dangerous situations such as abuse and rape. Looking back on it now, I can see how little by little and step by step, men violated what would've been normal healthy human boundaries, because I did not have them established as my boundaries. I had allowed men to dominate me by not being brave enough to defend the smallest of boundaries until it was too late.

With God, teaching me through Blaze, I learned that humans are just humans and with that comes selfish, sinful and sometimes dangerous behavior. That's who we naturally are. Yes, by God's grace, we can grow more aware of others' needs, and we can grow to be more self-sacrificing for others, but deep down inside, we are deeply aware of self and our self needs. That's why boundaries are so very important. They help others know what we deem acceptable in the way of interacting with us, and they help us protect ourselves from being taken advantage of, being bullied, or worse.

Probably the most important thing that I learned from Blaze is that establishing my boundaries must be done early on in relationships. Enforcing those boundaries calmly, patiently, and lovingly, helps compliance with boundaries be more effective. Anger only builds anger in others, then learning shuts down and the relationship is broken.

Scriptures do not tell us to never confront sin or wrongdoing. Actually, many Scriptures tell us that we must confront sin and wrong. However, it is to be done in balance with love and proper motives. Paul writes to us in 1 Corinthians 16:14 "Do everything in love" and in Ephesians 4:14 "Instead, speaking the truth in love, we will grow to become in every respect the mature body of him who is the head, that is, Christ." The Apostle John writes in 1 John 3:18 "Dear Children, let us not love with words or speech, but with actions and in truth."

Everything we do, but especially when dealing with opposition, needs to be done in the Spirit of love. We need to come to understand that "loving others" doesn't mean doing whatever the other wants. I think we all know people who do whatever they think another wants simply out of fear or even out of a motive of manipulation, themselves. It boils down to motive. Loving others is more than words, feelings, or actions. Any of these three things can deceive ourselves and others. It truly boils down to our motives and intentions. We can genuinely love someone while telling them something that they do not want to hear. They may get hurt and even angry, but that's okay; perhaps even necessary, if our motives and intentions are genuine love.

Oddly enough, by accepting people for who they are (even accepting their selfish natures) and by establishing healthy boundaries for myself, relying on the Spirit's wisdom to see people through God's eyes, I can love them more genuinely.

"Accepting" them doesn't mean accepting their behavior of violating my personal boundaries. The Apostle John states in John 2:24-25, "But Jesus would not entrust himself to them, for he knew all people. He did not need any testimony about mankind, for he knew what was in each person."

Although Jesus saw the value in all humans, was willing to heal and meet the needs of all humans, even dying for all humans, he did not allow himself to rely on them for camaraderie. He didn't allow himself to indulge in close personal fellowship with the masses. He knows us deep down inside and how fickle we can be. Jesus was able to love every human being so much that he was willing to die for every human being, however, he did not allow himself to depend on their love and faithfulness to be reciprocal. Even with the disciples he differentiated between those who were "coworkers" and those he considered true friends. Allowing those friends the spot in his most innermost circle; Peter, James, and John, he enjoyed close, personal fellowship, but even those, he knew not to depend too deeply upon. He knew their hearts. He knew that while they meant well, they were still human and could only give out of the resources that they had. We also, need to understand that some of our needs are too much for even our closest friends and family to meet. Those needs must be met by God, alone.

Personal boundaries are also a way for me to guard my heart and control my expectations of others. They enable me to allow people the freedom to be who they are, recognizing their shortcomings while loving them unconditionally because my love is based simply on who they are, rather than on expectations beyond their current character and abilities.

*Note: Early boundaries are essential for your personal safety. You need to be able to establish them immediately, "No, you don't have permission to get this close to me." "No, you don't have permission to touch me." You need to have resolve in your mind that defending your boundaries against things that make you uncomfortable is more important than potentially hurting someone elses' feelings or offending someone. By establishing these boundaries and defending them early, you may be able to avoid being in a dangerous situation. If the person does not respect the boundaries that you've established, they've indicated that you are, in fact, already in a dangerous situation.

Chapter 11

Where does Your Strength Come from?

I can do all things through him who strengthens me. —**Philippians 4:13**

Because of my history, I was the least helpful person in emergencies. I remember the time when Jenna had an accident falling off of Goldie. She was nine years old and she and I were riding in an open field. I was on Willow and she was on Goldie. I heard her screaming and looking back, I saw that she had fallen onto the ground. I went to her and found her hand contorted and beginning to swell. I immediately felt physically sick but forced myself to stay calm for her sake. For those already wondering, yes, she was wearing a helmet. Although I, myself, choose not to wear a helmet, I made sure that my kids wore them until they were adults and able to make their own choices. It turned out she shattered her elbow and broken her wrist in 2 different places. I was able to hold it together really well throughout her healing journey, up until the very end.

As the doctors were removing the pins from her elbow, I started feeling strange. The sounds around me began to be muffled, I started feeling confused and light-headed. That's all that I remember, until waking up on the floor with Jen looking down at me.

"Are you ok, mom?" she asked. *Wow. I passed out.* I said to myself. *What a great mom. I'm supposed to be comforting my daughter and instead, she's comforting me.*

I had been having panic attacks for at least the 6 years before this incident, although I didn't know it. They felt like chest pain, and I had difficulty breathing. I thought I was experiencing mini heart attacks. One time the pain and pressure in my chest were so intense that I went to the doctor to see if I was in fact, having a heart attack. The worst panic attack that I had was while I was driving. I had dropped Tim and Daniel off at youth group, and Dylan and Jenna off at the church for children's group, and decided to go for a drive down memory lane to one of my favorite places in my past where I would bike ride. It was a beautiful road and brought me such peace when I was on my long biking treks.

As I drove down the road through the towering pines on both sides, an uneasy feeling began coming over me. I started to feel confused about where I was. The uneasiness grew into terror. I can't explain what happened exactly;

all I know is that the terror that I felt told my body that I was in grave danger and that I needed to get out of there. I turned the truck around as quickly as I could and drove back to the youth group to pick up the older boys. Trying to talk to the youth group leaders, I was so confused and I was having difficulty enunciating my words. Also, I was speaking slowly because it took me a long time to think about what to say. I was so confused that I couldn't make sense of what they were asking or saying. I left there to go to the church where Dylan and Jenna were. The youth group leader called the pastor of the church because he met me at the door. Thinking my symptoms might be diabetes-related, he offered me some crackers and juice. Then he and his wife decided that they should drive me to the hospital. That's where it was discovered that I was having an anxiety attack. It was one of the most terrifying experiences of my life because it came on so suddenly without provocation, and it happened while I was driving.

I never had another anxiety attack that bad again, however, for the next 4 years or so, I had anxiety attacks nearly every night. Same scenario; I would be suddenly awakened in the middle of the night and sitting straight up, I would be sobbing and shaking uncontrollably in terror. Tony started "helping" me by telling me to calm down. That there was nothing to be afraid of. One time, in his frustration, he shouted at me to calm down. That only made things worse. Now, I had the stress of trying to make myself calm down to calm him down. The next day, I explained to him that this way of helping me was not helping me. I asked him to just pray over me from now on.

The prayers worked. Every time I would have a panic attack, Tony would start praying for me. After a few minutes, peace would settle over me and I would lay back down and fall asleep as suddenly as I had woken up.

These are the reasons why I was the least helpful in emergencies. Any event that created a high amount of stress in me would push me into a panic attack. Even if I could hold it together for the actual emergency, it was guaranteed that a panic attack was soon to follow. Most of the time, however, in emergencies, I allowed Tony to handle them, because my immediate response was dropping to my knees, sobbing and praying. A breakthrough for me came the day that Goldie had her first major accident and there was no one but me, to help her.

Goldie had developed the habit of pulling back from being tied and breaking her lead rope and/or her halter. I don't remember the exact day that she first did this; all I know is that from that day forward, that was her response to being tied. She broke 2 halters by the time I asked Kelee what I can do to fix this problem. Kelee suggested using two halters to tie her; one nylon halter and beneath it a rope halter, that way if the nylon halter broke, I'd still have the rope halter. The rope halter has knots strategically placed so that when a horse pulls against it, the knots apply pressure to the horse's skull. The horse then stops resisting in order to relieve the pressure. Not only that, but a rope halter is more difficult to break.

I tied Goldie to the side of the trailer, and sat next to her, reading a book aloud. I wanted to have her tied, but give her the assurance that I was right there so that she had no reason to be nervous. So far so good. I then walked several feet away and sat down under an oak tree. I was still within her eye-sight, and I figured I would sit down and continue reading the book to her. I would be further away from her, but close enough for her to be able to see and hear me.

She lasted for about 5 minutes. I watched her look around. "Easy baby," I told her. "You're fine. I'm right here."

I watched her slowly pull back as she'd done twice before. Stunned that the rope didn't break, she leaned forward, then I literally watched her squat her butt down and pull the rope! Well, it snapped that time, but I watched Goldie roll over onto the gravel road. I quickly ran to catch her and saw that landing on the gravel, she ripped her knee open.

I immediately started to panic. The first thoughts that ran through my head were, *Oh, no. I can't deal with this!" "What am I going to do?* I quickly assessed the situation in my mind. Tony was at work. I was it. I was the only one there that could help her. Psalm 29:11 states, "The Lord gives strength to his people; the Lord blesses his people with peace." Additionally, 2 Timothy 1:7 states, "For God has not given us a spirit of fear, but of power and of love and of a sound mind."

I took a deep breath. "Lord help me." I whispered in my mind. "Calm me down and give me clarity." Calmly I grabbed my phone to call the vet. No answer. I called every vet in my contact list and either they didn't answer, or they didn't make farm calls or the farm call would cost me as much as the actual treatment. I sent Kelee a message. Kelee told me to rinse the wound thoroughly with cold water from the hose. She said that this would help clean the wound, but also the cold water would reduce the swelling. She told me to send her pictures of what the wound looked like. After about 10 minutes of rinsing her wound, Kelee told me to wash the wound with diluted Betadine. I would have to gently scrub underneath the flap of hide that had been basi-cally, filleted back, in order to get any dirt and debris out. She then asked me if I had any antibacterial/antiseptic ointment. I told her that I had something called TriCare. She told me to apply it liberally to the wound, particularly to the flap of hide. It would keep the risk of infection down, and would also help keep the flap of hide soft and pliable, ensuring that it would heal back into the flesh around it. Otherwise, the flap would dry out and shrivel up, leaving that area exposed to heal. She told me that due to the area of the wound being her knee, this would probably take quite a while to heal

"You can do this." Kelee said to me. "It's really not that bad." Kelee then sent me pictures of a much worse wound that she had dealt with. Truth be told, I trusted Kelee. She was my hero. Honestly, I wanted to be like her, so her advice, guidance and encouragement was so important to me.

To my surprise, I stayed calm during the whole thing. Even pulling the flap up and sticking my fingers underneath to clean it out. After finishing, I stood up to just pause and reflect on what just happened.

"I can't believe it," I said to myself. "I did it. I handled an injury without hyperventilating!"

Goldie's injury healed beautifully. The flap of hide healed back to the surrounding tissue and there's only a little evidence of the injury. Her hide shows a "V" where it was torn, but otherwise, it healed together beautifully.

This experience was essential in my healing. It taught me that God has given me all the courage that I need to face whatever comes my way. All I need to do is take a deep breath and choose to rest emotionally in his peace and let his courage fill me.

I am amazed to wonder if when facing the cross, Jesus was perhaps (dare I suggest?) afraid? I mean, the human side of him. Matthew 26:39 states that Jesus, "Going a little farther, he fell with his face to the ground and prayed, 'My Father, if it is possible, may this cup be taken from me. Yet, not as I will, but as you will." This is also recorded in Mark 14:35, Luke describes the depth of concern Jesus was experiencing in Luke 22:44, "And being in anguish, he prayed more earnestly, and his sweat was like drops of blood falling to the ground." Matthew 26:42 describes Jesus' courage as he continues, "My Father, if it is not possible for this cup to be taken away unless I drink it, may your will be done." Imagine what he was facing. The physical aspect: excruciating torture, humiliation, and horrifying death of pain and asphyxiation. The spiritual aspect: all of humanity's sins ever committed and will be committed being placed onto him, momentary separation from God because of the chasm between sin and holiness, and the wrath of the Father and his punishment for all those sins being poured out onto him.

Hebrews 12:2-3 states, "For the joy set before him (Jesus) he endured the cross, scorning its shame and sat down at the right hand of God. Consider him who endured such opposition from sinners, so that you will not grow weary and lose heart."

Jesus was able to endure because he kept his eyes on the joy that was coming. He was able to face down the shame of a criminal's death on the cross, because of the joy that he knew his obedience to the Father would bring. I honestly believe that the reason for Jesus' joy was bigger than simply receiving a "well-done" from the Father, although that is what we all aspire to hear when we enter his presence. I believe that Jesus' joy, the prize that he kept his eye on as he obediently walked to the cross, was knowing what he was accomplishing for us. I believe that is key in helping us overcome certain trials, ourselves. At least, that has been the case for me. There have been some struggles that I have been able to endure more gracefully when I consider the good that may come to my family members from my patience in affliction.

I still struggle with anxiety, but it's becoming more manageable. I've learned that I need to keep in constant relationship with God daily in order to bathe my spirit in his peace. Reading the Psalms helps tremendously. First of all, the psalms disclose the raw honesty of the writer's emotions of anxiety, depression, and anger. I am greatly encouraged even if just for this reason, because it gives me relief knowing that I, too, can come to God with my raw, honest emotions. However, the psalmists also teach us how to change our perspectives in order to help influence our emotions.

I have noticed that I can't always trust my emotions. I may feel a certain way based on how I interpret what I'm experiencing through my senses, however, the information that I receive through my senses may be incomplete or possibly even wrong. For example, Tony may say something and immediately I may feel hurt. Then I might feel angry. I have learned to go to him and say to him, "I'm feeling really hurt" or "I'm feeling really angry because of what you said. I realize that I could be tired and could be hearing it with tired ears and a tired heart, but can you clarify for me how you truly intended for that to sound?" Granted, this level of communication is very time consuming, and Tony isn't always crazy about taking the time to process through things with me, but it has helped our relationship tremendously. It has helped him to understand me better, it has helped me to understand myself better as I learn how to dig down deep inside myself to figure out why I'm triggered and what's really going on inside of me, and it has also helped me to see how my emotions can't always be trusted.

The psalmists present their real emotions, but they also meditate on the past goodness and deliverance of God on their behalf. They trust God and believe in his future goodness and deliverance. Psalm 42:5 states, "Why, my soul, are you downcast? Why so disturbed within me? Put your hope in God, for I will yet praise him, my Savior and my God." I've learned to acknowledge the emotions that I'm feeling and additionally to challenge them. *Why am I feeling this way?* Or I tell myself, *Ok, I am feeling this way, but I have no logical reason for feeling this way, so I can't believe this feeling as the truth of my day right now.* Additionally, I've learned that practicing gratitude every morning helps me focus on how much God loves me and it reminds me of how he has blessed me.

1 John 4:18 states that, "There is no fear in love. But perfect love drives out fear." I've learned that if I concentrate on God's love for me, it helps me handle the bad things that happen. I can't really explain exactly how it helps, other than knowing that he loves me and knowing that I can trust him gives me peace.

I also learned how to listen to my body: learning where my stress threshold is, learning about my triggers, limiting how much stress I expose myself to, establishing boundaries so that I'm not over-committing myself, taking measures to reduce the stress as soon as possible when I feel it beginning to become unmanageable, adjusting the foods that I eat, and practicing deep breathing and calming techniques. I don't know if I'll ever be completely healed of it this side of eternity, but by God's grace, I'm so much better than what I was, and by God's grace, I'll continue to heal and grow.

I smile as I remember talking with a pastor about the heaviness of the sorrow I was going through. I remember telling him, "I can't take any more."

He said to me, "Yes, you can. You are stronger than you think. You have the strength of Jesus within you."

I remember thinking to myself, *Wow. Really? Thanks, I think. What an insensitive jerk. Doesn't he get it? I don't want to be strong enough to endure this. This isn't even fair that I should have to endure this.*

At the time, I resented his counsel. In my extreme heartache, I chalked him up as a male chauvinist, incapable of really understanding the wounds in a woman's heart. It wasn't until recently that I've come to appreciate that counsel from so many years ago. I've realized that life is pain. Yes, some people experience more suffering than others, but the reality is very few people escape this life without some scars. I have two choices before me. I can either fold up under the weight of the pain, or I can rely on God's strength to help me rise above the pain. One of my gifts is stubbornness (although Tony may not call it a gift). I am too stubborn to give in without a fight. However, I've learned a different battle strategy. Ephesians 6:12 states, "For our struggles are not against flesh and blood, but against the rulers, against the authorities, against the powers of this dark world and the spiritual forces of evil in the heavenly realms." I've learned to wage war through prayer and faith in God to defeat my spiritual enemies. I've learned to wield my sword while sitting on my Daddy's (God's) shoulders. Having survived some pretty significant battles, I have come to agree with that pastor and truly appreciate his words. He's right. I can handle anything as long as I'm relying on God for his strength.

God spoke to me through a dream one time about my role in a spiritual battle. In my dream I was facing Satan and his demons, as he was trying to attack a group of children in my care. I remember in my dream I was quoting

Scripture and proclaiming the name of Jesus. The demons were defeated, however, Satan was not. With each verse I quoted, Satan would disappear, but he would reappear behind me. I remember in my dream, feeling physically fatigued from running back and forth, standing between Satan and the children. In my dream, Satan laughed at me. This dream was so surreal and I woke up greatly disturbed. I couldn't understand why I couldn't defeat Satan in my dream. I prayed about it and God spoke to me and said, "Every battle is different and requires different battle strategies. He was taunting you and laughing at you because he was able to do what he set out to do. He was wearing you out."

I asked God, "So what should I have done differently?" He pointed me to Mark 9:14-29. The disciples were trying to cast a demon out of a boy, but they were unable to do so. Jesus cast out the demon and when the disciples asked him why they couldn't drive it out, he stated, "This kind can only come out by prayer."

God also pointed me to Ephesians 6:10-18. "Finally, be strong in the Lord and in his mighty power. Put on the full armor of God, so that you can take your stand against the devil's schemes. For our struggle is not against flesh and blood, but against the rulers, against the authorities, against the powers of this dark world and against the spiritual forces of evil in the heavenly realms. Therefore, put on the whole armor of God, so that when the day of evil comes, you may be able to stand your ground, and after you have done everything, to stand. Stand firm then, with the belt of truth buckled around your waist, with the breastplate of righteousness in place, and with your feet fitted with the readiness that comes from the gospel of peace. In addition to all this, take up the shield of faith, with which you can extinguish all the flaming arrows of the evil one. Take the helmet of salvation and the sword of the Spirit, which is the Word of God. And pray in the Spirit on all occasions with all kinds of prayers and requests. With this in mind, be alert and always keep on praying for all the Lord's people."

I noticed that the word "stand" occurred 4 times in the first 5 verses. Verse 13 caught my attention, stating, "Therefore, put on the whole armor of God, so that when the day of evil comes, you may be able to stand your ground, and after you have done everything, to stand." In my mind, I saw a battle going on. There was so much dust, that I couldn't see anything. As the dust cleared though, I saw myself. I was a pitiful, haggard sight. I was battle-torn, ragged, covered in dust, tears, sweat and blood, and breathing heavily. But... I was still standing with a sword in my hand hanging by my side. That's when I realized that maybe being victorious in battle doesn't always mean conquering all of my foes, but instead, simply being found still standing. Not knocked down. Not defeated, myself. That's what makes me victorious. I'm simply to be ready and able to stand my ground when he wages war against me and the way to stand my ground is best done on my knees in prayer.

Friend, whether you believe it or not, you are caught in the middle of a spiritual war. A war between God and Satan over the destiny of your soul. What's your battle strategy? May I be so bold as to suggest to you to take up your sword of the Spirit, which is God's Word? God's Word is Jesus, himself (personified). John 1:1 says, "In the beginning was the Word, and the Word was with God, and the Word was God. He was with God in the beginning." 1 John 1:1 also states, "That which was from the beginning, which we have heard, which we have seen with our eyes, which we have looked at, and our hands have touched; this we proclaim, concerning the Word of Life." Additionally, Revelation 19:13 states that "his name is The Word of God." God's Word is 2) every word in his Scriptures. Hebrews 4:12 tells us, "For the Word of God is active and alive. Sharper than any double-edged sword, it penetrates even to dividing soul and spirit, joints and marrow; it judges the thoughts and attitudes of the heart." 2 Timothy 3:16 states, "All Scripture is God-breathed and is useful for teaching, rebuking, correcting and training in righteousness." Friend, when you surrender your life to Jesus and live by the help of the Scriptures, you are able to confidently stand in the day of battle with God's sword of the Spirit in your hand.

Chapter 12

Faith, Hope, and Love

And now these three remain: faith, hope and love. But the greatest of these is love. **-1 Corinthians 13:13**

One evening, while going through the images of horses for sale, while sitting in bed, an image caught my attention. "Honey!! How much do you love me?" I hollered out to Tony.

"No more horses!" He hollered back to me from the living room.

"But, honey, look at this little cutie patootie!" I crooned over the image of a little mousey colored foal. Another picture included the foal's black and white mother.

"No!!" He emphatically retorted.

I crawled out of bed and went out to the living room and plopped right down next to him.

"Don't even think about it. I'm busy saving the world from a zombie apocalypse." He said to me, frantically pushing the buttons on his controller, eyes so intently focused on the TV that he refused to even glance at me. This was a risky move on my part.

"Just look!" I pleaded, opening my phone to a Facebook listing, showing him the picture of the cute little foal by its mother's side. Tony let out a big sigh and paused his game. "They're selling both the mare and foal for five Hundred and fifty dollars" I exclaimed. "I could train the foal and it'd be even better trained than Goldie because I've learned so much over the years!"

"No more horses. Especially since it is a twofer!"

"But that's exactly why we should get them!" I interjected. "Because it is a twofer!"

"No! Two mouths to feed, two to vaccinate, eight hooves to trim instead of four, and two more potentially expensive vet bills. No, No, NO! Besides, what the heck would we do with a shetland pony?" He was quite adamant and laid a convincing argument.

I swooped in on the opportunity. "She's already trained to ride. See? Here is a video of her being rode. She'd be perfect for the grandkids." Unwavering, Tony propped his legs back up onto the coffee table, preparing to resume saving the world. I knew that I was losing influence. "Can we at least go look at them?" I asked, pressing my face directly into his line of sight, batting my big, brown eyes at him and pursing my lips into the most pathetic, irresistible pout I could.

"Fine, I'll humor you and we'll go look at them, but that's it. I'm telling you right now, that we're not buying them."

He lifted the controller and as he pushed the play button, I said, "Whew! That's great because, I already told her that we'd come to look at them on Saturday." Tony's mouth dropped open, but before he had a chance to pause his game again, I jumped up, "Thank you honey! I love you!" I bounced off back to the bedroom.

"We're only looking!" He yelled back to me. "We're not buying anything!"

"Yes, dear." I hollered back to him from the bedroom, while settling in under the blankets.

Saturday arrived, and I had the trailer hitched to the truck. "I thought we agreed that we weren't buying them." Tony said as he came out of the house, a cup of coffee in one hand and a bottle of soda in the other.

"Yes, of course," I said, taking the soda from him. "But it's always a good idea to be prepared." Tony grunted while getting into the driver's seat.

"Why do I always seem to get hoodwinked? It's a good thing I pulled out cash, too, I suppose." I looked over at him, surprised. "One can never be too prepared." He said to me with a wink. "But I'm not paying her asking price. I pulled out exactly the amount that I'm willing to pay."

Oh, Lord, if this is your will, please let her sell them for exactly what's in Tony's pocket. I prayed to myself.

We arrived at the farm and greeted the gal who was selling them. The shetland mare and her foal were standing quietly tied to a hitching post. Already a good sign that they were trained to stand tied.

"The mare had been used as a ring pony at fairs. A girl I know bought her from a guy who owned a pony ring business", the owner said to me. I was working on lifting the mare's feet to see how she reacted to having her feet handled. Before I could make my way to the back feet, the girl interrupted me. "She's touchy about having her back feet handled." She wasn't kidding.

The mare's hips got tight and her rear end looked like the hammer of a gun being cocked back and ready to fire. I removed my hand out of fear that the next movement would be the mare launching herself over the hitching post.

"Ya wanna see the sire of the foal?" the owner asked us.

"Sure!" I said, curious as to the other set of genes that the little one inherited.

As we walked over to another pasture, she began telling us the mare's story. "The girl called me and asked me if I would take her horses because her boyfriend was getting pretty abusive to them."

My heart sunk. *Could that explain why the mare was so tense about having her rear feet handled?* I wondered to myself.

"We took the sire and the mare. At the time, she hadn't foaled, yet."

Well, that's good. I thought hopefully to myself. The foal likely hadn't had any bad human experiences, then.

"Here he is." she said, pointing to a beautiful large buckskin appaloosa. "Go on in and meet him if you'd like. He's calmed down a lot since he's been here." She invited us.

"Holy moly!" I said to her while standing near the huge stallion. "That little mama had a baby sired by this guy?"

"Yes ma'am."

"I can't believe he's so calm and well mannered." Tony chimed in.

"So how old is the foal?" I asked. "And is it a filly or a stud?"

"She's a little filly and she's only a little over a month old."

We patted the big boy, admiring his beauty and his calm disposition for a little while longer. "Can I see someone ride mama?" I asked.

"Sure thing." she responded. There was a blonde young lady that was standing by the mama and the filly when we got back to the hitching post. "Would you hop on and show them how she rides?" The owner asked the girl.

"Sure. I just gotta get her bridle." The blonde disappeared inside the barn. After placing the bridle on the mare, she jumped on bareback and rode her down to the end of their driveway and then back. I was impressed.

"What's the lowest price you'll take for them?" Tony asked, true to his policy of never giving anyone their asking price.

"I'll take five Hundred dollars," she responded. "I can't go a penny less."

"Well, that's perfect, because that's how much cash I have on hand." Tony replied, reaching into his wallet.

Yes! Thank you, Lord!" I shouted in my mind.

Once the money exchanged hands, we untied mama from the hitching

81

post and walked her over to the trailer. She loaded like a champ! She stood calmly tied inside the trailer as we went out to fetch the baby. I could hardly contain my elation. *Yay!! I'm gonna have another baby to play with!* I thought to myself. The little foal hopped right up next to her mama and we closed the dividing gate. After lifting the ramp and closing the exterior gate, we thanked the girl and began driving away.

"That was entirely unfair. You know that, right?" Tony said to me as we headed down the road.

"What do you mean?" I asked him.

"You knew I wouldn't be able to resist that cute little thing, didn't you?"

"Oh, come on. A tough military guy like you, getting all soft over a little foal?" I chuckled.

"So, what are you thinking for names?" Tony asked me.

Hebrews 11:1 came to my mind. "Faith is confidence in what we hope for." At this point in my life, I needed an increase, spiritually, of both faith and hope. Perhaps this was God speaking to me, through these two horses. I felt strongly that their names were supposed to be "Faith and Hope", but which name for which horse was unclear to me.

"Well, for mama, I think we'll call her 'Faith' and for baby, I think we'll call her 'Hope'". I didn't know then; how significant those names would be for each of them and how God would use those names to teach me about them.

We got the pair home and had to leave them in the trailer while we figured out where we were going to put them.

"We really don't know how Goldie and Blaze are gonna react to having these two here." I told Tony. "And I've heard of stallions killing foals. Granted, Blaze is a gelding, but he has always acted "stud-y.""

We ended up using the round pen within the pasture as a way of introducing them. Faith and Hope would be kept safe by the round pen panels, while Goldie and Blaze got to know them. Once we got the pair unloaded and settled into the pen, I attempted to pet Faith but I couldn't get near her! The round pen was just large enough for her to continue moving away from me. I tried everything that I could think of to coax her to come to me. I tried waiting until she was standing still, and calmly quietly tried to approach her. I tried being inconspicuous by walking sideways and even backwards! Nothing worked. Every time she sensed that I was approaching her, she would move away from me. Eventually, she got to the point where she was running around the round pen from me! Worse, she was teaching Hope to run from me! This was terrible! All I wanted was to hug them and welcome them into our new little family, yet, here she was, rejecting my love. How can we bond if she kept avoiding me? It was then that I got the first glimpse of how much work was cut out for me. It was also the first glimpse of the truth that God had planned to teach me through them.

For the next few days, I changed my approach. Instead of going out to the round pen, with the expectation of petting them and loving on them, and forcing the building of the bond, I decided to just go out and sit with them. I needed to go out and just observe them. Maybe by watching them and how they interact and react in my presence, I can gain some insight into their personalities.

Each day I would go out to the round pen with a book, sit on a rock and read quietly while watching them. At first, Faith was wary of me and insisted on keeping Hope from being near me. For a few days, seeing that every day, I simply shared space with them, Faith seemed to loosen up a bit. She still avoided coming near me, but I sensed that she was moving from fear of me to apathy for me.

It made me think of myself, and others that I've known who've experienced hard things. Sometimes, the best intentions of people to "fix" things, or "make you feel better" actually make a person feel worse. Maybe you can relate. You can feel "rushed" in working through the complicated emotions of the situation. Sometimes the situations are so confusing, that working through the understanding of them takes time, and feeling rushed adds to the confusion and anxiety. Sometimes, the most helpful, loving thing that someone can do is to just sit with you and share space with you.

Hope, on the other hand, was curious. Honestly, this was what I was expecting from a foal with no prior negative experiences with humans. Each day, Hope continued to grow in her curiosity of me and soon began displaying playful behavior. Faith grew in her indifference to me. It seemed as though she no longer saw me as a threat, which is why she allowed her foal to explore me, however, she still wanted nothing to do with me.

I experienced my "aha" moment when I read somewhere that faith is a complete trust or confidence in something or someone. Faith is best when it's grounded on facts and trusts in those facts. In my shetland pony's world, the facts that her faith was grounded on was that humans were dangerous and couldn't be trusted. She was sold multiple times, so even non-abusive environments didn't last long enough to change her mind set about the danger of humans. At the very least, it stunted her ability to bond with humans.

Hope, on the other hand, is built on faith. It is the confident expectation that naturally stems from faith. The more that I worked with my little filly, Hope, the more I was fascinated with how different she was from her mama. Hope seemed to have no fear. For a few months, she grew to seemingly enjoy spending time with me and she was willing to trust me and do whatever new activity I presented to her. Even going into the house with me!

Hope's willingness to follow wherever I led her was her expressing her faith in me. Her faith was built on complete trust in me. Now, she could live out her name, having a confident expectation of a relationship made of safety and love.

We, humans, rely on our 5 senses to give us facts about the things going on around us. Those facts make up what we know as our reality. However, the facts from our senses can't always be trusted. This is where we can let ourselves get stuck. When our faith is in our senses and they tell us that our situation is so dire that there's no reason for hope, we can find ourselves drowning in an ocean of despair. In the ocean of despair, we either lose ourselves in depression, or we destroy ourselves with shallow and counterfeit happiness such as addictions. Because our senses cannot give us insight into the spiritual realm, we believe an incomplete reality. Understanding the existence of the spiritual realm and the spiritual battle that we're in, we can accept that there are aspects unknown to us, that can change our true reality.

When our faith is grounded in an all-powerful God (even though he may be largely unseen), we can begin to believe that there is the possibility of more going on that we do not see. When our faith is grounded in the God who loves us and makes all things work out for the good of those who love him (Romans 8:28), it is the anchor of hope that keeps us from drowning in the ocean of despair. Our faith in God gives us hope that the impossible is possible.

I honestly believe that this was a mistake that I had made when Dylan and Jenna were going through their toughest trials in adolescence. Having studied psychology and counseling in college, and using that education to work through my own issues, I was pushing Dylan and Jenna into practicing what I had learned. I strongly believed that the sooner you face your problems head-on and work through them, the sooner you get to heal from them and experience the peace you need to move on.

What I didn't take into consideration was that Dylan and Jenna were still kids. They were in their early teens and so much was going on for them. We had just moved from Bemidji to Fort Ripley only a couple of years before that. Truth be told, we moved a lot in their short lives. I took for granted how hard change can be for kids especially change in homes and schools. Making friends was hard because of the time that it takes to make friends. Then, with each move comes the loss of those friendships. Tim told me many years later that a consequence of my choices to move so frequently was that he developed a fear of making meaningful relationships because he hated the loss of those relationships.

You add in a new "man of the house" (Tony) with new expectations and new family dynamics along with the changing and confusing hormones of puberty, it is a lot for any young person to manage. How I wish I knew then, what I know now. I wish I would've known the importance of simply sharing space with them instead of increasing their stress and anxiety by pushing them so hard through their healing. Being overwhelmed with all the confusing emotions that they were dealing with, all that I had accomplished was pushing them away.

I learned several years later that there is a big difference between developing healthy ways to cope with the trauma from your past and actually being healed from the trauma of your past. We can learn how to manage our behavior and our thought processing to cope with our trauma, but that it is only like applying a splint or a cast to a broken leg. It helps us get back to walking, but we're walking with a limp. Healing comes from God. Psalm 147:3 states, "He (God) heals the brokenhearted and binds up their wounds." Healing from God comes when we allow him to share space with us. It comes from baring our hearts to him and pouring out our pain to him and then simply letting him love us back to wholeness. God's love is the healing balm for our souls.

As a mother comforts her child, so will I (God) comfort you. —Isaiah 66:13

Imagine a crying child being held tightly by his/her mother. Whispering, "shhh, it'll be alright", she rocks her child back and forth. She hasn't done anything to change or fix the problem at that moment. She isn't giving long explanations for why this happened or how things could have been done differently. She isn't using this as a teaching moment for emotional or intellectual growth. There is a time for that, but in the pain, what brings the child security and comfort is simply being held, comforted and loved. It is exactly how God heals us if we'll let him. Many times we resist his healing, perhaps without even knowing it. In our panic, we just want to know "why?" Or maybe we want God to just fix it and make it better. As the Creator of our souls and spirits, God knows that explanations, facts and even the love from other people (or animals for that matter) aren't enough to heal us. Only absorbing his love for us can truly heal us.

Healing is a process that requires time and consistent "space sharing" with God. How many of us have deep wounds that feel better after just a few chats with our best friends? I would say that's near impossible. For many of us, it takes years for some wounds to stop stinging. God is so good and works so patiently on us. He knows us so well and knows the perfect pace at which we can handle his carefully peeling back of the scar tissue that has developed over our wounded hearts.

I (God) will sprinkle water on you and you will be clean; I will cleanse you from all your impurities and from all your idols. I will give you a new heart and put a new spirit in you. —Ezekiel 36:25-26

Believe it or not, our pain can become an idol for us. Some of us have experienced so much trauma in our lives that it becomes our identity. Without even realizing it, we may function through life with a "victim" mentality or conversely a "fighter" mentality. The survival skills of avoiding threats or fighting back against threats may have been necessary for past circumstances, but we can get stuck there; functioning from those positions out of instinct with no real threat at all.

God wants to change our hearts. He wants to remove the timid spirit that functions simply for survival and give us a spirit that thrives. Perhaps this is you, friend. Perhaps you require some healing balm applied to your heart. Isn't it time to share space with God and let him love you into wholeness?

Chapter 13

Ya Just Gotta Have Faith

Faith is the confidence of what we hope for and assurance about what we do not see. —Hebrews 11:1

Faith is such a cute little black and white Shetland pony. I love how she adds color to our little herd. However, she adds much more than just color. Faith teaches me every day. Ever since the day that we brought Faith home, she has puzzled me and put me into a position to constantly think. In fact, God has used her many times to teach me about myself. Faith is one of the most interesting horses that I have encountered and I've had trouble with knowing how to build a relationship with her. It's hard to have a relationship with someone who doesn't seem to want a relationship.

It is interesting to me that once she's caught, she is the most obedient horse that we own. She loads into a trailer wonderfully. She stands while being tied; yes, she may be nervous, but I've never had her try to pull back and break the rope or halter. She stands for grooming. She leads and backs. She listens so well, intently watching her handler and responding accordingly. However, there was one area in which she didn't behave so well: that was standing when the farrier was around to trim her hooves.

Any time I had Kim, our farrier, out to trim hooves, I always saved Faith for last. From the minute that she was caught, Faith would tremble at the feeling of a hand on her. It was so strange for me having a horse that seemed to hate being touched. Most horses are calmed by a gentle touch, but Faith trembled. If you tried touching her face, ears, sides, belly, and particularly her feet, she tried to move away from your touch. If she couldn't move away, then she would warn you that you were at risk of being bitten or kicked.

Things were particularly difficult a year after we bought her. Building a relationship with her was so tedious. It was always one step forward, eight steps back. For over a year, I tried to build a relationship with her, with results so minimal that I don't even know if I can say that I saw results. Then she came down with "scratches".

I still don't know a lot about what "scratches" is. From my understanding, it's a bacterial/fungal infection that enters through breaks in the skin and causes clusters of sores on the legs. From my understanding, it mainly affects only the rear legs, however, it has always affected all of the legs on Blaze and now, Faith. A person better be treating them at the first sign of them, because it progresses rapidly and is extremely difficult to get under control and it is very painful for the horse.

I had learned from treating Blaze, that I had to break down the treatment process into very tiny steps. Blaze also, was very difficult to treat at one time. He was never aggressive about it, but he wouldn't stand still long enough for me to be able to treat him. It got so bad that if I just looked at a leg, half bent over, he'd start moving. So, I had to break it down to looking from a standing position, if he didn't lift a leg, then I'd tell him "good boy" and then I'd look away for a few seconds. Then progress to bending over. If he didn't move a leg, I'd stand up, praise him and look away. This made the progress of treating him so slow, but it is what I had to do if I wanted to be able to finally get a rag on those legs to clean them and treat them.

Faith was a tougher case. I had no positive foundation of trust to build on, she already hated having her feet touched, and it seemed like the "scratches" exploded at once. I tried the technique that I'd learned from Blaze, but she wasn't buying into it. I spent hours every day, trying to get her to let me just get close enough to look at her legs. Finally, the "scratches" were getting so bad that I knew it was time to just do something. I tried tying her to a post, thinking that she's always been compliant while tied, I'll just have to go in and scrub her feet whether she likes it or not. It is for her own good, and besides, how hard can fighting a little pony be? I found out that a little pony has a lot of fight. Don't let their little size fool you.

So, then I decided to tie her in a little stall, hopefully confining her movement. It's astonishing how powerful the rear end of a little Shetland pony is. I was out of breath and sore from her whipping her butt around and pinning me against the walls. The worst part of all this was that this whole scenario destroyed the little bit of trust that she had in me. We were worse off than when we started.

I decided it was time to call the vet. The vet came out and sedated Faith then shaved her legs and treated the "scratches". I was relieved to have them cleaned, but I knew that I had to continue treating her legs or they would come back. It was no use. The trust was eroded and the best that I could do was tie her to a post and quickly spray antibacterial spray onto her legs from a distance and before she could react. Over the next few days, I saw evidence that the "scratches" were coming back. There was nothing more that I could do than what I was already doing, so I prayed every day that God would just help get rid of them.

God did get rid of them and she has not had them again, since! Because of her episode of having "scratches", I realized that I needed to be more intentional about working with her, touching her all over, particularly her feet.

I learned a lot about Faith. Since providing affirmation through touch was not effective, I had to find something else. I found out that Faith loves treats! I trained the horses to come to me when I whistle a special sound. Once she realized that the special sound meant peppermint candies, she would come running with the others whenever I would whistle that sound. Then I started to change things up a bit. I started alternating between candies, apples and carrots. Faith loved them all. So, I took the lesson that I learned with Blaze and broke down the process into tiny steps. I tied her to a post, and if she let me touch her without flinching, I'd stop and give her a treat and then walk a few feet away, standing with my back towards her. I wanted to take away any physical or psychological pressure from her. Then I would come back and spend a little more time on that particular spot. If she flinched or moved away from my touch, I would try again until the second that she didn't flinch. Then I would give her the treat and walk away. I had to do this with everybody part that she wasn't comfortable with me touching. Her ears, her face, her chest, her flanks, her belly. I didn't attempt this on her feet at this time. This was a very long, tedious process, but I started seeing progress and was elated.

One day, I was calling the horses to me, handing out treats and just petting them. Everyone had their treats and I was making my way around petting everyone. My other three horses thrive on attention so they stick around long after the treats are gone, although they continue to sniff my pockets to make sure that the treats are REALLY gone. I took a few steps towards Faith and she took a few steps towards me, stretching out her neck and sniffing. I held out my hand, walking very slowly towards her, hoping in my mind, "Maybe we've built enough relationship that she'll finally let me approach her and pet her." No such luck. She sniffed my hand and realizing that there were no more treats, backed up and walked away.

I watched her intently. It made me so sad. No matter how much I tried to build relationship with her, she wanted no relationship with me. Without treats, there was nothing that I had to offer her that she wanted. Then God gently spoke to me through that moment. "Kiddo, now you know how I feel." *Ufdah*. It reminded me of what Jesus said to the crowds in John 6:26, "Jesus answered, 'Very truly I tell you, you are looking for me, not because you saw the signs I performed but because you ate the loaves and had your fill.'"

How many of us are at the end of God's lead rope and we're obedient to him simply out of our physical need or even compulsion? We don't really trust him, though. In fact, we tremble if he tries to know us too deeply. God pursues relationship with us as passionately as I pursue relationship with Faith, yet how many of us treat God like Faith treated me? Only going to him for the treats in his hands, satisfied with a shallow knowledge of him and our limited understanding of his expectations. Keeping our noses to the ground, doing what we believe we're supposed to do, expecting a quid pro quo system

89

of rewards for our obedience, and if he doesn't deliver, we back up and walk away, wanting nothing more to do with him. How many of us go through life doing this or doing that, trying to prove to others around us, ourselves, maybe even God himself, that we're good enough? We wear ourselves out trying to perform a certain way. We wear ourselves out emotionally, trying to "be" a certain persona. Trying to change ourselves or "make" ourselves someone that we're not, is exhausting. On top of it all, if our hearts are wrong, the rewards that we get from simply obeying or following all of the rules, are temporary. They're only good while we're on earth.

As Jesus taught in Matthew 6:1-7, "Be careful not to practice your right-eousness in front of others to be seen by them. If you do, you will have no reward from your Father in heaven. So, when you give to the needy, do not announce it with trumpets, as the hypocrites do in the synagogues and on the streets, to be honored by others. Truly I tell you, they have received their reward in full. But when you give to the needy, do not let your left hand know what your right hand is doing, so that your giving may be in secret. Then your Father, who sees what is done in secret, will reward you. And when you pray, do not be like the hypocrites, for they love to pray while standing in the synagogues and on the street corners to be seen by others. Truly I tell you, they have received their reward in full. But when you pray, go into your room, close the door and pray to your Father, who is unseen. Then your Father, who sees what is done in secret, will reward you."

Jesus continues speaking to the crowd in John 6:27, "Do not work for food that spoils, but for food that endures to eternal life, which the Son of Man will give you. For on him God the Father has placed his seal of ap-proval." The people in the crowd ask him in verse 28, "What must we do to do the works God requires?" Verse 29, "Jesus answered, 'The work of God is this: to believe in the one he has sent.'" That sounds pretty simple! I find it quite astonishing that the next thing the crowd does is ask for a miraculous sign so that they might believe in him. He just got done doing miraculous signs that they benefited from, including miraculously feeding them to their fill! That's why they're following him, to begin with!

They venerated Moses and so used him as an example of how he delivered their ancestors from Egypt and while on their way to the promised land, fed them heavenly bread called manna. Jesus corrects them and tells them that it was God, not Moses, who provided them with the bread, just as God is providing bread of life for them now. Verse 34, The people eagerly reply, "Sir, always give us this bread." Jesus declared in verse 35, "I am the bread of life. Whoever comes to me will never be hungry, and whoever believes in me, will never be thirsty."

As you read further, the people were offended by this teaching because they thought he was speaking literally. However, he's speaking of spiritual hunger and spiritual filling and spiritual life that is for eternity. Matthew 5:6 explains what Jesus is saying here. "Blessed are those who hunger and thirst for righteousness, for they will be filled." When Jesus becomes the most important thing to us, we begin to "feed on" him by absorbing as much of him as possible through the Scriptures. We begin to seek his guidance in every aspect of our lives. We begin to seek his comfort in our struggles, his love when we feel lonely, his strength when we feel weak. He becomes our sustenance and will provide everything that we are lacking. And ultimately, he is our source for life eternal after physical death.

When we get our sustenance for spiritual living from him instead of trying to squeeze it out of our own limited resources, we are able to do what God requires and live according to his expectations without feeling depleted.

In John 4:32 Jesus tells his disciples, "I have food to eat that you know nothing about." He explains further in verse 34, "My food is to do the will of him who sent me and to finish his work." He's saying in a sense, that obedience to God is what fuels his existence.

I looked back at Faith and back on the years that we've owned her. At this very moment, she is standing off by herself eating grass away from the others. She doesn't even desire a relationship with the others in her herd. Truth be told, she was always pushed around by everyone else in the herd. Everyone else gets to eat, drink, roll, or find shelter first. If she is in the way, everyone will pin their ears back and stretch their necks out towards her, indicating to her that she had better get out of the way, and quickly. Even her own baby pushes her around. Hope isn't mean about pushing Faith around. She's just significantly bigger and more exuberant, so in her haste, she ends up pushing her mama around. Faith seems settled in her place of always being last, always moving out of the way. She doesn't fight for a higher position. She just stays out of everyone else's way, off by herself to avoid conflict. The only time I'd seen her aggressive towards any one of the other horses, was when Hope was just a foal and Faith felt she had to defend Hope. She's also gotten after Hope for being a little too aggressive while nursing. How many of us go through life like that? We believe the lie that we don't matter to anyone. Our needs wants, desires and dreams don't matter. We will always be at the end of the line so why bother trying to change our circumstances? We reluctantly accept the lies as truth and give up. Don't get me wrong; as I said in a previous chapter, each member of the herd needs to know her place. We need to have a willingness to be content in our current circumstances, but I think we need to have a balance between being content and being open to new possibilities. That's what helps us feel alive! Dreams, goals, ambitions, well, HOPE is what gives us that gleam of life in our eyes, even while being content in our current circumstances.

Looking at Faith, I could see myself in my present life. Overall, I was safe. Tony was never abusive to me, but because of my history, and because of painful experiences in our current marriage, I was like Faith. I was content staying where I was, but I didn't desire a close relationship. To avoid conflict, in order to avoid more hurt, I had built emotional perimeters around my heart. I was capable of leaving the perimeters if I chose to, but no one was allowed into the innermost perimeter, not even my husband. My relationships with others take a long process to build, much like the process between Faith and I. I don't readily seek out relationships with others, and any deep, personal relationships that might evolve from say, work or church relationships, take a long time. At the first scent of potential rejection, I tend to pull away from those relationships, needing to step back and assess when and if the time comes to where it is safe to take a step back in. Maybe you share a similar personality. Have you been wounded in such a way that you've erected walls of safety around your heart? Do you avoid close relationships with other people and perhaps even God, himself?

I have been working on trying to tear down my perimeters, but honestly, it is terrifying to me. Those perimeters keep me safe. However, God has shown me that those same perimeters prevent me from having deep, meaningful relationships with him and with others.

I also saw similarities between Faith and I in her obedience. As I said before, on the lead line, I cannot believe how obedient Faith is--until she feels threatened. She does what she's supposed to do because it's expected of her, as long as it doesn't threaten her. She's willing to be obedient to a certain point. God has healed me and helped me get to the point where I am obedient to him because I love him. However, much like Faith, I am obedient to a certain point. When obedience threatens my physical or emotional safety, then fear overtakes me and I resist being obedient. I have seen myself, as Faith, either trying to run away from God or pulling away from him, maybe even trying to bite or kick in my efforts to get away.

1 John 4:16-18 tells us, "And so we know and rely on the love God has for us. God is love. Whoever lives in love, lives in God, and God in him. In this way, love is made complete among us so that we will have confidence on the day of judgment, because in this world we are like Him. There is no fear in love, but perfect love drives out fear, because fear has to do with punishment. The one who fears is not made perfect in love."

To love God is to obey him, the two greatest commands are to love God with everything we have and to love people with the same love we have for God. In order to obey Him with a pure heart, we must love Him and rely on the knowledge of His love for us. Knowing that He loves us fiercely, gives us the confidence to act in obedience to Him. We are able to love others despite our fear because the knowledge of God's perfect love for us, gives us the security of being able to risk rejection from loving others unconditionally. Obedience to God cannot come from fear of punishment, because that is not true love. Obedience to God comes from the love we have for Him after receiving the love that He has for us.

I have not reached this ability to perfection, yet, but through the power of the Holy Spirit, I continue to grow day by day. By the grace God gives me each day, I am more courageous in my love today, than I was a five years ago, and by the grace of God, I will be more courageous in my love five years from now than I am today.

Recently God has shown me a very important truth that I hadn't realized before. He asked me, "Why did you buy Faith? What is your purpose for her life with you?"

I thought about it for a minute, and I said, "Well, I bought her as a riding partner for the grandkids."

"Is she a trustworthy mount for them?"

"Well, no. Not yet, but she's getting there."

"What do you see as the main barrier?"

I thought about it for a minute, and said, "She still doesn't trust people. She's come a long way with me, but she is still very wary of anyone else."

"So, although she has grown in her trust in you, you still expect that she will grow into a reliable, trustworthy mount that will take care of your grandchildren. That's your purpose for her, right?"

"Well, yeah."

"That is the expectation that I have of you, as well," God said to me. "My purpose for rescuing and purchasing you is that you would grow in your love and trust in me, but also that you would grow in your love of my children and grandchildren and take care of them. Your fear and mistrust are preventing you from really loving people the way I want them to be loved. let's be honest, there are times when you even use fear as an excuse to not have to love people as deeply as you know you should. If we're honest, there are some people that you really have no desire to get to know so that you can show them my love. Isn't that true?"

Ouch. I pondered this for a moment and searched my heart. I asked my-self, *what am I really feeling in certain encounters with others?* I found that God was right. There are some people that to love them, it requires stepping outside of my comfort zone and risking rejection. There are others that to love them requires stepping outside of my comfort zone and taking an active interest in them, even when I have no interest whatsoever. In other situations, it means being willing to sacrifice my neatly planned out day to make time for another person. "I'm sorry, God. You're right. I can be a very selfish, self-centered person, can't I?"

"It'll be ok." God said to me. "You aren't planning on giving up on Faith, are you? You're going to keep working with her to grow her into the pony that you intend her to be, right? Well, I'm not giving up on you, either."

God is so good and patient with us. Psalm 103:13-14 states, "As a father has compassion on His children, so the Lord has compassion on those who fear Him; for He knows how we are formed, He remembers that we are dust." Each of us is a work in progress. You, my friend, are a work in progress, and Paul assures us in Philippians 1:5-7 that God will continue His work in us until it is completed when Jesus returns for us.

Loosen your reins and relax in the saddle. We're halfway home!

Chapter 14

Trust Doesn't Come Easy

Trust in the Lord with all your heart and lean not on your own understanding; in all your ways submit to him, and he will make your paths straight. —**Proverbs 3:5-6**

One day, as I was leading Hope from the pasture to the trailer, I was beside myself with joy "Oh! I'm so excited!!" I said "This is so exciting, honey! You get to go on your very first adventure with me!" Hope just plodded along, unaware of the whole thing. She and I had a wonderful bond. She was used to being introduced by me to all sorts of strange things, like the time when as a foal I led her into the house, or the other time, when I walked her up and down the handicap ramp of the house that we were renting. It was wonderful having a little foal, again. Of course, it helped that she had a personality similar to Goldie's. Hope, just like Goldie, was my little buddy. She followed me wherever I went, genuinely curious as to what I was doing and where I was going. However, I realized the errors of my ways in treating Goldie like a lap dog and was intentional about not making those same mistakes with Hope.

Because Hope was very similar to Goldie, I set out on doing some things differently. I had learned a lot about boundaries over the years and set my mind to teaching them to Hope right from the beginning. I wanted to teach her right from the beginning that while I love her and want to enjoy a close affectionate relationship with her, it's required that she respects me.

So here we were, getting ready to go to a training facility for a day activity. This would be an important milestone for building confidence in Hope. She was now 3 years old and this would be the first time that she spent any significant amount of time away from her mother. I chose not to wean her and allow her mother to determine when the right time to wean her would be. This trip would be a perfect first step. The training facility was only about 8 miles away and it would only be for a few hours. So, she wouldn't be away from her mama long and then she'd be right back. Additionally, this would be only the third time that she'd been trailered and the first time on her own. This would be a huge first step for her, but in my eyes, it would be an easy first step in comparison to what my long-term plans of training were for her.

Hope's trust in me enabled her to follow easily and she loaded without hesitation. I tied her to the front of the trailer. Another lesson I had learned from Goldie was that allowing her when she was still young to turn around in the trailer had become problematic when she grew as she had gotten too big to do that. Then I had the struggle of retraining her to NOT turn around and stand tied. I really didn't want those kinds of problems with Hope.

After going around the trailer several times to ensure that everything was closed, we were ready to go. As we headed down the driveway, there was a lot of whinnying between Hope and her mama, which I expected. I figured that after we got further down the road, Hope would calm down. She didn't. I felt the trailer rocking back and forth as she anxiously danced back and forth. I was thankful that she wasn't a full-sized horse and just a large pony.

After we got a little over a mile down the road I pulled over to check on her. As I peered into the slates of the stock trailer, I could see that she was trembling. I reached my hand out to pet her. Her eyes were wide with fear. "Hey. It's ok, honey. I know that this is scary, but you're ok. I'm right here." I spoke softly and gently to her, hoping to calm her down. "We don't have far to go. It'll be ok." I jumped down from the side of the trailer and began walking back to the truck.

In my spirit, I heard God say to me, "She can't see you, so she doesn't know that you're "there" for her. She has to learn what you've had to learn. To trust what you can't see." I felt goosebumps all over, but I didn't have time to ponder and process, I had to get going or we'd be late. In order to minimize the trauma on Hope of trailering, I wanted to drive slowly.

We arrived at the training facility and I found a place to park. I shut off the truck and checked on Hope. The poor thing was so scared that she was dripping with sweat. "Oh, baby, it's really not that bad." I sighed. "I'm gonna just let you stand here and calm down."

I heard God speak to me in my spirit, "Kandy, don't you see? This is you. You still struggle with trusting me. You get overwhelmed and your fear takes over. Your anxiety gets you so worked up that you suffer physical ailments." Again, more goosebumps and I felt disturbed, but again, I didn't have time to process and ponder all of this.

I went around chatting with a couple of the other clinic participants and gave Hope a chance to just calm down. I also checked out the obstacle course for the clinic. I was surprised at all of the different, creative obstacles that were available. However, I was unsure as to what Hope's frame of mind was, this could be a challenge.

I went back to the trailer and saw that Hope had calmed down, so I unloaded her and walked her to the barn. The trainers were a husband and wife team. The husband took Hope and tied her to a rail. This would be interesting. Hope had learned how to "give" to pressure and I had worked on having her stand tied before. However, it was only for short periods and I was always within eyesight of her. I was apprehensive about leaving her alone, but she was tied securely and within a pen, so even if she broke loose, she would still be contained.

After a short briefing on the obstacle course and the outline of the day, all the participants went to get their horses. Everyone else rode through the obstacles. I was the only participant there to work solely from the ground. There were so many intriguing obstacles. There was a "curtain" of noodles for the horses to walk through, a "box" lined with tarp and water inside for the horses to walk into, a plastic kiddie swimming pool with water, several tires for the horses to learn to maneuver through, large, sand-filled tractor tires to step up on and stand on, several large tractor tires filled with sand that simulated a mountain to climb, a wooden "bridge" to cross, a wooden "teeter-totter" to walk across, a "ramp" whose rails had balloons on both sides that you had to walk through, a large trench, and many others.

To be honest, everyone was impressed with how calm and well-behaved Hope was and how well she walked through all of the obstacles with only minimal hesitation; especially after they heard that this was the first time away from her mother and her herd, first time trailering alone and the first time that she'd been to a clinic.

After we'd gone through the obstacles several times and it appeared that Hope was bored, I took her into the round pen to see if she would play with a giant horse activity ball. She didn't seem interested. So, then I decided to free lunge her and try to "join up." Hope had been lunged on a lunge line before, but never free lunged in a round pen, so she had no idea what "joining up" was. She followed my directions perfectly, and when I turned my shoulder to her and knelt, she walked right up to me and placed her muzzle on my shoulder. I was moved to tears. Looking into her face and seeing the gentleness, I knew in my heart that she loves me and I love her.

Around noon, the trainers said it was chow time, so the other riders put their horses away and I left Hope in the round pen to relax. We all sat around and ate and got to know one another better. After I was done eating and chatting, I decided that it was time for me to get Hope home. Once again, she followed my lead and loaded without hesitation. After watching her intently through the rearview mirror for a couple of miles down the road, my eyes filled with tears. There was no bouncing around in the trailer, no incessant crying out. She was standing calmly, almost contently. It was as though she grew up and was no longer afraid.

I heard in my spirit, God saying to me, "She needed to overcome her fear of the unknown. As her leader, you took her from everything she knew to somewhere that she didn't know she was going. She couldn't see you even though you were there with her the whole time. You knew where you were taking her, and you knew that it would be good for her. You knew the big plan that you had for her. It was a good plan, a plan of enjoying a relationship of adventure with her, but she had no way of knowing your plan. Her mind wasn't created to comprehend what your mind can. You arrived at your destination and she was able to see you again. You led her through scary obstacles, but she knew that you were right there beside her to help her. She successfully navigated all of the obstacles and realized that she was safe. This experience increased her confidence in herself and her trust in you and consider how everyone marveled at your relationship. Look at her back there, she's so relaxed that she's almost falling asleep. This was a lesson as much for you as it was for her."

We've got to come to a place where we can trust in the Lord with all of our hearts, just like Hope trusted me and followed me into the trailer. Trust begins through establishing a relationship. In relationships, we get to know others. We learn about their mannerisms and patterns of behaviors. It takes time with frequent, close interactions to learn about one another. We learn how people respond to stress, we learn about what their values are, we can learn if they're capable of commitment or if they avoid commitment. Through time, we can see consistencies in how they behave and those consistencies create a bedrock of trust.

Establishing a relationship with Jesus is very simple at first. We just ask him! Maintaining that relationship, just like any relationship, is more difficult. It requires sacrificing time to do what we want to do in order to spend time with the other. In our relationships with Jesus, we spend time getting to know him through reading the Bible, prayer (which is simply conversation with Jesus. You speak to him as you would to any of your other friends. You tell him what's on your heart, and then you listen for his words), and inviting him into all of your activities. As I've discussed in previous pages, one of the ways that I've grown in my trust in Jesus is through experiencing his deliverance in my sorrows.

It is a strange paradigm. Going through difficulties, shook my trust, but strangely, stepping out in faith in God, and later, experiencing his deliverance, increased my trust! As hard as it was going through those things, I'm thankful for those experiences, because they created a way for Jesus to do the impossible, thus increasing my trust and faith in him. This is where it's important that we don't lean on our own understanding because our understanding is limited, just like Hope's understanding of where I was taking her was limited.

God's perspective has been explained to me like this: imagine that you're in a hot air balloon or a blimp and you're hovering above the Thanksgiving Day parade (That's one of the nation's largest parades each year). You're able

98

to see everything; the parade route, the beginning of the parade that has already reached the end of the route, the middle of the parade-making it's way to the end, all the way to the end of the parade where the floats and participants are still staging to begin the route. You can see the crowds of people, the cars, the buildings, etc. You can see everything happening, in progression, all at once. This is a rudimentary example, but this is sort of how God sees life on earth. Because he is outside of time and space, he can see all of life on earth, from the beginning to the very end all at once. This is the reason that we must rely on his guidance and not on our limited understanding because he has a perspective that we do not. He sees the dangers ahead of us that we do not see. He also sees the outcomes that we're not able to see.

An example of this is found in Exodus 13:17. "When Pharaoh let the people go, God did not lead them on the road through Philistine country, though that was shorter. For God said, 'If they face war, they might change their minds and return to Egypt.'" God changed their direction, because he could see the danger ahead and knowing the emotional and physical states of his people, he also knew how they would potentially react to the danger ahead. God knew that they were not ready to face war, yet. So, in his mercy, he directed them away from that danger. The people didn't have the insight that God had. All they knew was that they were wandering in a hot, desert, for a very long time, taking the long route. Not knowing that God was saving them from a battle that they were not prepared to face, they grumbled about what they saw as unfair and unreasonable circumstances. They were so disgruntled that they even wanted to go back to their lives of slavery! They didn't understand that their hardship of taking the long route was actually an act of mercy and protection.

Have you had moments that you can relate to them? I know that I've been guilty of this. I remember distinctly, moments where God gave me something that I had been begging him for, but it was harder than I imagined it to be. After some time, I began grumbling about the difficulties of the very thing he gave me and even stated that I would rather go back to…X, Y, Z! Or I made statements like, "Even…X, Y, Z wasn't this difficult!"

Thankfully, God has nurtured me to a point, where I am able to recognize and acknowledge these thoughts more quickly. I repent of them and make a conscious effort to thank God for the blessings and ask him for the strength and courage to do what he has called me to do.

The thing is, God also allows each of us to have free will. We have the freedom to choose whether we will trust him and follow him, or trust our own intellect and hearts. We've already discussed why we can't fully trust our intellect, but what about our hearts? The world's advice in making decisions is for us to "follow our hearts", however, Jeremiah 17:9 states, "The heart is deceitful above all things and beyond cure. Who can understand it?" The fact of the matter is, that we humans have a hard time knowing ourselves truthfully. We lack the ability and insight to draw out the true motives in our hearts and consider them impartially. Even if we gain that ability and insight, it takes tremendous courage to face the truth of who we are.

I the Lord search the heart and examine the mind. —Jeremiah 17:10.

God is the only one who can know the truth in our hearts. Thankfully, he is compassionate to us, so he exposes the truth to us in love. His goal in exposing our hearts is not to destroy us but to transform us. For God to be able to transform us, we need to submit to him and allow him to guide us in the necessary changes. As we submit to His authority and allow Him to change our hearts, our minds and our wills, we are better able to discern the paths that he's leading us on. And this is where life gets truly exciting.

Lean forward, squeeze with your legs and hang on! It's a steep incline to the top!

Chapter 15

Faith Over Fear

Therefore I tell you, do not worry about your life, what you will eat or drink; or about your body, what you will wear. Is not life, more than food, and the body more than clothes? Look at the birds of the air; they do not sow or reap or store away in barns, and yet, your heavenly Father feeds them. Are you not much more valuable than they? Can any one of you by worrying add a single hour to your life?
—**Matthew 6:25-27**

I'm sure that you have situations that cause you concern. How do you feel in those situations? How do you handle those situations? A beautiful image of faithful trust occurred to me when Tony came home from work one night. While he was changing his clothes before going out to take care of the horses, I watched all four of the horses run from one part of the pasture and stand near the water tank at the other part of the pasture. It was kind of funny actually, staring out the window and seeing all four of them staring back towards the house. It was almost as if they knew that the house was our "barn" and they were waiting for us to come out and feed them. Honestly, it was humbling as well, knowing that our horses have that kind of faithful expectation of our care of them.

This morning, it was my turn to go out and feed the horses. The same scenario; as soon as they heard the front door open and close, they ran from one part of the pasture to wait for me near the water tank. I considered this; how they truly depend on us for all of their sustenance and they are so confident in our care of them, that at the moment that they hear the front door, they know that we will be there with food for them.

I try to be as consistent as possible regarding feeding times, but to be honest, with our work schedules, they may not get their first servings of hay until the afternoon. It doesn't appear to matter, though. As soon as they hear the door open and close, or as soon as they see our presence, they run with an expectation to the water tank.

It made me think of my relationship with God. Psalm 8:4 says, "What is mankind that you are mindful of him? Human beings that you care for them?" Psalm 55:22 says, "Cast your cares on the Lord and he will sustain you, he will never let the righteous be shaken." Psalm 144:3 Lord, what are human beings, that you care for them, mere mortals that you think of them?"

God has proven to me time and time again, that he cares for me and provides for all of my needs. However, like the horses, there are many times that I have to wait on God's timing for His provision.

It really gives me great comfort in knowing that just as it is my responsibility to care for the needs of my horses without regard to how they perform, as a child of God's, He assumes the responsibility for caring for my needs regardless of how I perform. Therefore, I don't have to be anxious when God tarries in providing for my needs, because I have the assurance that He will. I just have to trust Him enough to keep watching and listening for him and be ready to receive his blessings.

Cast all your anxiety on Him because He cares for you. —1 Peter 5:7

Don't be fooled, though. I haven't yet mastered this. When things seem impossible, my first reaction is to worry, but I've learned to press the "pause" button in my mind. I tell myself to take a deep breath and focus on deep breathing. I tell myself, "You have been given a choice. You can choose to worry, or you can choose to give these concerns to God and wait on him." As Paul writes in Philippians 4:6, "Do not be anxious about anything, but in every situation, by prayer and petition, with thanksgiving, present your requests to God." I try to practice this myself, telling God my concerns, and telling him that I trust him with those concerns. Throughout the day when those worries creep back into my mind, I remind myself, "I'm choosing not to worry about this because I've handed this over to God." Don't get me wrong, I don't mean to say that faith gives us a license to be lazy and not take care of our responsibilities, or plan. Genesis 2:15 tells us that God intended for humans to work from the very beginning. "The Lord God took the man and put him in the garden of Eden to work it and take care of it. "This was before Adam and Eve sinned, so working the garden wasn't a curse from their sin. I believe that it was another way that we are created in God's image. God worked on creation for six days. On the sixth day, he saw that everything was good. I believe that God wants us to have something to do so that we can experience the joy of accomplishment. God worked for six days and on the seventh day, he rested. He provided work and rest for us. We don't fully appreciate rest until our work creates a need for rest. It wasn't until after Adam and Eve sinned that God cursed Adam saying that because he sinned, the ground was cursed and that his work would be hard (Genesis 3:17-19).

Proverbs 20:4 says, "Sluggards do not plow in season, so at harvest time, they look but find nothing." What the writer is saying here, is that lazy people who don't work, won't have food to eat. Paul writes in Thessalonians, "For even when we were with you, we gave you this rule: 'the one who is unwilling to work, shall not eat." Again, Paul writes in 1 Timothy 5:8, "Anyone who does not provide for his relatives, and especially for their household, has denied the faith and is worse than an unbeliever."

Throughout the Scriptures, we are shown the expectation of having a balanced life of faith in God's providence and personal responsibility. We learn that balance by asking God to help us prioritize our lives and let him tell us what we should be doing in each situation. Honestly, that is where I've found a tremendous amount of peace. When we listen for God's direction and follow that direction, it eliminates a lot of stress, because we can know that we're within God's will. We don't need to stress because we know that we're doing what we're supposed to be doing and trusting God for the rest. Because of God's great love for us, we can trust him to provide for our needs.

Chapter 16

A Shared Load is a Lighter Load

Take my yoke upon you and learn from me, for I am gentle and humble in heart, and you will find rest for your souls.
—**Matthew 11:29**

Ayoke is a device for joining together a pair of draft animals -especially oxen-, usually consisting of a crosspiece with two bow-shaped pieces, each enclosing the head of the animal. The purpose of the animals being yoked together is for pulling carts, wagons, carriages, or farming implements. When a person yokes two horses together, they have to be perfectly matched and trained to be able to pull together. If they aren't perfectly matched and aren't trained, they will pull against one another. Only by working together, can they successfully pull a heavy load. And by working together, the work is easier.

It's astonishing to discover what Jesus is saying when we consider this in the context of Matthew 11:29. I believe what Jesus is saying is that when we give our lives to him we are joined with him (yoked with him). With him helping share the load, we will find rest because we won't be bearing the load by ourselves. However, we must learn to stay in step with him so that we aren't pulling against him, else the load becomes more difficult than it needs to be.

Horses are living and breathing beings with their unique personalities. The plans that I have for my horses go against their very nature. It is not natural for them to have devices placed on their bodies and in their mouths. It is not natural for them to have a two-legged creature directing their every move, especially into situations where their natural instincts are to panic and run to safety. It is not natural for them to carry a creature on their backs (in fact, in the wild, a creature on their back meant they were probably going to die).

For them to become obedient to my directives that go against their instincts for self-preservation, trust in me is required. How do I prove myself trustworthy to them? I have to have clear expectations of them. I have to be patient as I teach them my expectations and I have to be consistently firm but gentle and fair in my correction of mistakes

The philosophy of my horsemanship is that we are a partnership. I want to make sure that as much as possible, they want to partner with me in my goals. Yes, essentially, I am the boss, so to speak, and I need to be the one in control. I need to know that my horses will obey. If they are unruly and diso-bedient, then they are unpredictable and dangerous. So, I need them to re-spect my authority, but my ultimate desire is a partnership. This means that I have to do everything in my ability to make sure that I have first and fore-most, taught them what I'm asking them to do and that they've demonstrated capability in doing what I've taught them to do.

Additionally, I want to make sure that what I'm asking them to do is as easy, relaxing, and enjoyable for them as possible. I want them to enjoy spending time with me. I want them to enjoy the adventure of trail riding and exploring new places with me. I want them to know that some of the ad-ventures may be challenging, but they can trust me to get them safely back home. I've been taught that in training and communicating with horses, you "tell" the horse that they've gotten the right answer by removing pressure from them.

In the early years of owning her, I recognized that for Faith, my touch was physical and emotional pressure on her. I had to learn to touch her just long enough before she would move away; before the first visible sign of dis-comfort, then I would remove my hand. I wanted a relationship with her which required touch, but I also wanted her to trust me. I wanted her to know that I wasn't a threat to her and that my touch would not be used to hurt her. I knew that I had no right expecting cooperation from her until I had estab-lished trust with her. I couldn't build trust with her until I had proven to her that I respected her. Because of Faith's background, she had a lot of trauma to overcome, so respect for her means being sensitive to her trauma.

Once I recognized that Faith no longer viewed me or my touch as a threat to her safety, I began to increase my expectations of her. It was time for her to start demonstrating her trust in me by taking baby steps of simple obe-dience. My expectations of obedience are different for her than say, of Goldie. Goldie and I have 15 years of relationship under our belts, so I expect more from her than I do of Faith. I know what each of them is capable of. I know what their weaknesses are and what areas we need to work on, so when I work with them, although the end goal is the same for all of them -to be trustworthy mounts- the progression of getting to the end goal is different for each of them depending on where they're at each day.

I believe that God looks at each one of us this same way. The end goal is the same for all of us: to have faith in Jesus, living eternally with him in heaven and progression in Christ-like growth. However, because we are individuals with different backgrounds, personalities, and abilities, the pro-gression for getting to the end goal is different for each of us. God knows where we are in life and how best to instruct us.

And he (God) passed in front of Moses, proclaiming, 'The Lord, the Lord, the compassionate and gracious God, slow to anger, abounding in love and faithfulness, maintaining love to thousands, and forgiving wickedness, rebellion and sin. —Exodus 34:6-7

Isaiah 42:1-3 states of God's coming Messiah (Jesus), "Here is my servant, whom I uphold, my chosen one in whom I delight; I will put my Spirit on him, and he will bring justice to the nations. He will not shout or cry out, or raise his voice in the streets. A bruised reed he will not break, and a smoldering wick he will not snuff out." Throughout the Scriptures, we read that God has compassion for his people. He knows that when he rescues us and brings us into his pasture, some of us come with trauma. He knows that he may have to spend years, moving slowly and methodically towards us before we can accept his touch. He knows how much intimacy we can handle. He knows how much pressure to apply, in the right measure, and when to remove the pressure to increase our trust in him.

God expects obedience of all of his children, just as I expect obedience from all 4 of our horses. Just as I know the areas in which my horses need growth, God also knows each of his children's areas that require growth. He deals with each of us individually, and he knows that for some of us before he can expect obedience, he first has to ensure that we feel loved, respected and safe.

We have to understand this also when dealing with people, ourselves. Some people that we meet may come off as abrasive or "stand-offish". I've been a person who "moves away from" others. Not wanting them to come too close in physical proximity but also in emotional proximity. I've also known others who've done the same. It is possible that the behavior being displayed is from trauma and we just need to be patient, gentle and understanding; giving them time to build trust in us.

One day, not too long ago, as I finished giving the horses hay, I knelt in the snow looking at Faith and began talking to her. She turned her head and looked at me as she ate her hay. She stretched out her neck and I breathed into her nostrils, and she inhaled my scent. This was huge and moved me to tears. I've been told that horses breathing into one another's nostrils is equivalent to saying, "Hello! How are you today?" It's how horses greet one another. For Faith to stand where she was and turn to me and inhale my breath was huge in our relationship! Although it had taken four years to get to this point, she is showing that her trust in me is growing.

God is wanting to breathe life into you, are you willing to stretch yourself and inhale the breath of his Spirit? If you're worn out and weary from the loads you're pulling in life, won't you consider becoming yoked to Jesus so he can help you share the load? If you're already yoked to Jesus, are there areas that need to be surrendered and where you can learn, to become more evenly matched with Jesus so that you and he are pulling together?

We're heading down the hill, so lean back and give your horse his head. He knows how to navigate his way down and get ya to the bottom safely.

Chapter 17

Refreshing Waters

The purposes of a person's heart are deep waters, but one who has insight draws them out. —Proverbs 20:5

All of the commentaries that I've read regarding this verse explain it from the perspective of a wise person having the ability to draw out the purposes within the depths of another person's heart; as in the case of helping a struggling friend who's having difficulty opening up. Additionally, God gives us wisdom in discerning spiritual things and will sometimes help us discern what may be going on in another person's heart. Jesus tells us in Matthew 7:16 and 20 that his disciples are to watch out for wolves in sheep's clothing, and the way that we can discern the difference is by their fruit. John also writes to us in 1 John 4:1, "Dear friends, do not believe every spirit, but test the spirits to see whether they are from God, because many false prophets have gone out into the world." However, I believe that God prefers our focus to be on ourselves; and so, I believe the Proverbs 20:5 verse is a direction to ourselves to discern the depths of our own hearts.

Proverbs 16:2 states "All a man's ways seem innocent to him, but motives are weighed by the Lord." Proverbs 17:3 also states "The crucible for silver and the furnace for gold, but the Lord tests the heart." Again, Proverbs 21:2 "All a man's ways seem right to him, but the Lord weighs the heart."

When I first introduced Goldie to water, it was quite the ordeal. A former co-worker who used to work with Danny, Tony and I, had invited me to go riding with her. Sue and her husband owned a farm that bordered county land, so we would mount up at her farm, head off her property, and then ride out onto the county land.

Along the trail, we approached a significantly large mud puddle. Sue's horse, Lady, walked right through it. Goldie, however, stopped dead in her tracks and stared at the puddle. I tried to urge her forward but she refused.

Sue said to me, "Just let her smell it and look at it. Because of the way they see, when horses first see water on the ground, it looks like a bottomless hole to them, and they're afraid to step into it." We waited. "I'll bring Lady back through and stop her in the middle of it. Maybe Goldie will be more comfortable then." Sue brought Lady back through and Lady stopped to drink from the puddle.

I again tried to urge Goldie through. She wouldn't budge. "Try walking her back the way we came and approach again. As you get closer to the puddle squeeze with your legs to keep her sped up so that she understands that she has to keep going. See if that helps her walk straight through," Sue advised me.

So, I turned Goldie around and followed Sue's direction. As we approached the puddle, Goldie kept her pace, but she went straight up onto the edge of the trail, to walk around the puddle. I began getting frustrated at this point. "It's ok." Sue encouraged me. "It is best not to get into a struggle. If she's not ready to cross water, and you try making her before she's ready, it could go bad. We can try again on the way back home. Maybe coming from the other direction will be different." Sadly, it was no different. This continued to be an obstacle for the next few years. I remembered all that Sue had taught me, so whenever I was out riding and we came across a large mud puddle, I would work with Goldie with the advice that Sue gave me, but always with no success.

Then one day, I was out riding with a new friend who lived nearby. Angela knew of trails within the nearby Foothills State Forest, so I picked her and her horse, Dolly, up and we drove to the campground at the ski trails. The trails were beautiful and the landscape was diverse. Angela had been to these trails many times in the past and was very familiar with the area.

"Boy, it's pretty warm, today. There's a lake not too far from here." She told me. "Let's take the horses down there to get something to drink and cool off."

I gulped hard. I knew how much Goldie hated water, but maybe she would drink. We got to the lake and Angela rode Dolly straight into the lake. Considering that I can't swim, I really didn't want to take Goldie into the lake, but I did want her to drink, so I urged her forward. Goldie approached the lake apprehensively and got close enough to smell it. Apparently, she was hot and thirsty because she stepped forward with her front feet in the edge of the lake and took several long drinks. Then she surprised me! She walked right out into the lake and began wading in the water!

"You'd better make her turn around," Angela told me as she stood off to the right of me. "There's a sudden drop off over there." She said pointing out a route in front of us.

I was confused about how I felt about this situation. I was excited over this new experience and terrified at the same time. I turned Goldie back towards the shore, but she wanted to stay in the water! She began pawing the water with her front feet, splashing us. I was giggling at the sight. By this time, Angela and Dolly had gotten out and were standing on the shore watching us. Goldie began walking in circles and pawing the water.

109

"Uh, oh! You'd better watch…" Angela didn't have a chance to finish her warning to me. Goldie dropped into the water down to her knees! I was in the water up to my knees! She was practically lying down in the water! I was laughing so hard by the time Goldie stood back up. Riding bareback, I nearly slipped off while we were under the water, but after she stood back up, I was able to shimmy myself back into position. It was such an amazing experience and after we got back onto shore, I was so grateful to Angela that she had recorded the whole event. From that day forward, I never had any problems with Goldie crossing water. She loves the water! In fact, she loves the water so much that I have to be careful that she doesn't try to roll in every body of water that we're in!

Looking back on my life, I see that I followed a similar pattern, spiritually: the things that I've experienced have helped shape my personality. So, I've gone through life, just kinda doing what I knew. Reacting to situations based on how I've felt about the situations. Heavily relying on my gut and intuition. Things that seemed threatening to me, I avoided because it was too scary to confront. Honestly, looking back, most of my life, I was driven by fear. I didn't know it at the time. Even those choices that I made that were harmful to myself, were from a heart of rebellion and fear. A fear of never being happy, a fear of never being loved, a fear of never being "enough".

It wasn't until I reached a point in my life where the heat of my poor choices was wearying me. I was dry and parched and needed spiritual refreshment. That's where God drew me out of my shallow superficial thinking and out into the deep waters of truth: not to drown me, but to cool, refresh, and teach me. He first bathed me in the depths of His grace showing me just how deep His love is for me. Then in His wisdom and gentleness, He began taking me into the depths of my heart, revealing to me the truths of my faulty thinking and replacing it with His truths for me.

It is a terrifying thing, digging down deep into myself, challenging myself with questions like, *Am I really who I think I am? Do I really think this way about myself, and others?* I tended to like to hide behind masks. I tried to be a good person (overall). Who doesn't want to be seen as a "good" person? Before giving my life to Jesus, I did the best that I could to be a good role model for my children while they were in my care. When they were with their father, however, that was a different story. I did whatever I wanted. I partied excessively and was promiscuous. I justified my choices by saying that as long as I kept this part of my life hidden from my children, what was the harm? *I'm not hurting anybody else, what's the harm? Why should my personal choices for entertainment make me a 'bad' person?* I didn't realize it at the time, but I was living a life of continual lying to myself and everyone else around me. I was a different person to everyone I was around, depending on the context that I was in. Additionally, I was constantly looking for ways to make my "goodness" negate my "badness". It's no wonder I didn't know who I was. To be honest, I don't know if I really wanted to know who I was. Not until God took me out into the deep waters and showed me the truth deep within my heart.

Paul writes to us in Romans 12:2, "Do not be conformed to the pattern of this world, but be transformed by the renewing of your mind. Then you will be able to test and approve what God's will is--his good, pleasing and perfect will." Additionally, he writes in 2 Corinthians 10:5, "We demolish arguments and every pretension that sets itself up against the knowledge of God, and we take captive every thought to make it obedient to Christ."

God exposes the depths of my heart, not to shame me or belittle me, but to bring to my attention the lies that I'm telling myself and to drive those lies out in the light of his grace. Through a relationship with Jesus, he gives me new messages of love and grace, for myself and others. By changing the messages that I listen to, I can change my thoughts. By changing my thoughts, I can change my perspective. By changing my perspective, I can change how I handle my emotions and thus my behavior. When I have a mind set on God and Godliness, I can see things better from God's per-spective (certainly not perfectly, because His knowledge is too vast for us). When I can see things from his perspective, I can see that his way truly is the way that works best for my life.

By illuminating the dark motives deep within my heart, and replacing them with Godly motives, little by little He is transforming me into a person that I can honestly and genuinely love. I don't have to hide behind a mask of protection, afraid of knowing myself and being known by others. What about you, friend? Are you tired of feeling dry and parched? Maybe it's time to take a leap of faith and let God quench your thirst with His refreshing Spirit.

Chapter 18

Back to Basics

Let us hold unswervingly to the hope we profess, for he who promised is faithful. And let us consider how we may spur one another on toward love and good deeds. —Hebrews 10:23-24

As believers, we have a hope that encompasses both our temporary reality on earth and our eternal reality in the future. We are being exhorted to hold fast to that hope, on the basis that God Himself is faithful. The basis is not on our own faithfulness, because we have moments where our faith wavers. The basis is on God's faithfulness, which does not waver. Additionally, in holding fast to the hope we profess, we are to actively encourage our fellow believers to love others and do good to others. I believe the biggest barrier to loving people by doing good to them and for them, is fear.

I find it interesting that the writer of Hebrews chooses the word "spur". In the horse world, a spur is a little device worn on a rider's boot heels and used to encourage or urge a horse to move forward. It is as if the writer knew that we would have times where we needed someone who will aggressively urge us to continue in forward.

If ever there was a time when the world desperately needed courageous love and good deeds from others, it would be now. COVID-19 has turned our world upside down. Life was normal one day, and the very next, the whole world was on lockdown. What a strange way to live: where we were not supposed to leave our homes unless we had to -such as going to the store for "essential" groceries and supplies or our jobs-. We had to have papers in our vehicles stating that the government had deemed our particular employment "essential" so we were authorized to be on the roads. All businesses except those deemed "essential" were shut down for several months. Schools were shut down. Churches were closed down. Even parks were closed down and closed off. Because of the panic, people were mass buying products, creating a shortage.

COVID-19 brought out a side in humanity that I hadn't really seen with my own eyes, before. Sure, I'd seen selfishness in certain individuals, but never had it been on such a large scale, before. I cannot believe how common anger and even hate for others over simple disagreements have become, simply because people are afraid.

I'm not going to lie. It has made me afraid, too. My fear is not of COVID itself, but of not knowing what the truth is. Not knowing who or what to trust, what to do, or how to keep my family safe and together. Additionally, how do I love others the way that God wants me to?

The current events right now include the COVID pandemic and its accompanying loss of freedom, worldwide violence and riots due to racial issues, increases in domestic violence, increases in suicides, uncertain economy, and child sex trafficking on massive scales even perpetrated by some of the most elite and powerful of our world, among other topics. To be honest, I can't even believe that I'm living and seeing this. It truly is bizarre to be living in a state of such calamity and uncertainty even from day to day.

All this being said, feeling overwhelmed with fear and hopelessness myself, I needed the peace of a nice quiet ride; so, Tony and I decided to go for a ride around the square. The "square" is a 3.5-mile loop up the gravel road, down a minimum maintenance road, back onto the gravel road, and ending back to our home. This is where we do most of our riding.

Instead of riding Blaze, Tony decided to ride a bike with me. I was so moved by this gesture because Tony has bad knees. Too much walking causes him a lot of pain. Bicycling is even worse for him. It was a beautiful day for a ride and Goldie was doing great, as she always did. I was riding as I always do, bareback and bitless.

As we were on the home stretch of the minimum maintenance road, I saw ahead of us some ATVs facing us. I told Tony to ride ahead and ask them to slow down so that Goldie wouldn't freak out. The ATV riders shut their engines off for us and as I approached the group of about 6 or 8 ATVs, I noticed that one of the riders was a friend of mine. Tony had chatted briefly with them and was already rounding the corner, heading for home. I began chatting with my friend so Tony turned around to talk more with the guys. Goldie was getting prancy, but nothing seemed alarming, so I lingered, talking with my friend. Goldie continued to get impatient, and as we started to say our goodbyes, one of the ATV riders started his engine and his radio blared. Goldie snapped. She tossed her head and swung her body around. I jumped off because I know all too well what that means. It means she's had enough. She wants to go home NOW! She backed up and the lead rope reins were ripped from my hands. I tried to approach her to remove the reins but she backed up a few feet away from me. Her eyes were wide as she planted her feet.

I tried talking calmly to her, "Whoa, Goldie. You're ok." Then she launched herself straight forward and bolted past me, running for home. This was really bad. She didn't let me get the reins disconnected, they were still looped and hanging underneath her neck. I knew the danger of what could happen. If she somehow got her leg caught in that loop she could break a leg, her nose, her neck… "Please God protect her." I prayed. I told Tony that he needed to ride the bike to try to catch up to her. I followed behind, hurrying as fast as I could being barefoot on the sharp gravel.

An ATV flew past me from the direction that I was headed for. I shuddered at the thought of him flying past Goldie. "Oh, God, please let Goldie be ok." A truck flew past from behind me. "Oh, God, he doesn't know that we have a horse loose on the road and that Tony is on a bike. Please protect them."

Shortly after, Tony approached me driving one of our trucks. I hopped into the cab. "Is Goldie home? Is she ok?"

"Yeah, she's home, but you're gonna wanna look her over."

I was physically sick, imagining what injuries she may have. Once we pulled into the yard, I could see that Tim, was holding her lead rope and she was frantically grazing. "She just ran right up to me," Tim said as I walked towards them. "The clip broke off one side of her reins and she's got a few scrapes on her nose."

I looked at her nose and instantly knew what happened. *She must've gotten a leg caught in the reins after all,* I thought to myself. *That must be how the clip got broke. Oh, her poor nose! Taking the brunt of all that pressure.* We put salve on her scrapes then I took her halter off her.

"Tim, will you stay out here and be my spotter? I've got to get back on her for both my sake and her's." I asked him. So, with Tim standing by, I remounted her and decided to use the reins as a neck rope instead of having anything near her face. I rode her in a small area in our back yard. All things considered, she did very well and was overall compliant. That's all that I wanted, so we put her back out into the pasture.

A couple of days later, I decided that Goldie and I needed to get out for another ride. I figured that we needed to get back to normal as quickly as possible. After mounting, I was pleased to see that she was listening well and things truly seemed normal; so, we started on the driveway up the dirt road. We made it as far as the neighbor's house when she started balking. No matter what I did, she was not going forward. I tried backing her, I tried doing circles, I tried doing serpentine patterns; nothing was going to work. Every time I faced her back towards the direction away from our home, she planted her feet and refused to go forward. I knew it wasn't worth getting into a power struggle over so I got down.

"Goldie, we need to work through this," I told her. "That's fine if you don't want me to ride right now, but we're still going for a walk." I decided to hand walk her halfway around the square and then try remounting for the remainder of the ride home. Things were going well with Goldie and me, so I decided to try to mount before the halfway point. I stopped her alongside some fairly large boulders and remounted her. She began tossing her head and swaying back and forth. I had her stand still, but I could tell that she wasn't just still. She was tense. She tossed her head again and swung her butt around. I knew I needed to get off again. I lunged her both directions and stood her near the boulders again. This time she began pushing her head past me, as if to say, *Don't even think about it. I'm not letting you get on me.* For the first time in a long time, I was scared of her again. "Goldie, I know that you're upset with me. I failed you. I know, and I'm sorry, but we gotta work through our issues," I said to her. "It's fine. Today we'll just walk around the square together."

As we started out walking, I asked God what to do. He said to me, "Don't you see how you behave the same way? Scary things happen on the trail of your life and you panic. Instead of pausing and listening to my calming voice, you bolt forward and react. You become overwhelmed with fear of the unknown. Sure, we enjoy close fellowship when you remain within the safety of your comfort zone, but once you're outside of your comfort zone, you become unsure about whether I'm really reliable or not."

"Yeah, you're right," I said back to God. "So, what do I do to restore my relationship with Goldie?"

I heard God say to me, "Go back to the basics." I pondered over that for a minute. I was reminded of Psalm 42:6, "My soul is downcast within me; therefore, I will remember you (God) from the land of Jordan, the heights of Hermon--from Mount Mizar." The psalmist is dealing with his sorrow by remembering the landmarks where God provided miraculous deliverance. Again, Psalm 77:10-12 states, "Then I thought, 'To this, I will appeal: The years when the Most High stretched out his right hand. I will remember the deeds of the Lord; yes, I will remember your miracles of long ago. I will consider all your works and meditate on all your mighty deeds." Psalm 119:52 goes so far as to state that the writer is comforted by meditating on God's ancient laws.

I realized that during my hardest trials when I was confused about what God's purpose was for the pain, I needed to go back to what I knew. No matter what was happening and that none of it made sense, I knew that God loved me with a fierce love. I knew that he makes all things work together for my good. I knew he was with me and that he'd get me through it and our relationship would be stronger on the other side of my pain. I had to hang on to those truths as my anchor. I've also come to understand what the psalmist meant when he stated that meditating on God's ancient laws brought him comfort.

God's laws are moral boundaries for us, similar to the fence that I have for my horses. My horses may long to run free, outside of the fence, but the fence is meant to keep them in and safe. It is also meant to keep danger out. As long as my horses stay within the perimeter of the fence, they are safe and they have the assurance that I will provide everything they need. If they leave the safety of the fence, they run the risk of being in danger and lose the assurance of my ability to provide for their needs.

God's moral boundaries for us guide us to safety and away from danger. When we stay within the perimeter of those boundaries, we have the assurance of God's protection and providence. That's not to say that nothing bad will happen to us even within the perimeter of God's fence. Just like things happen to my horses within the pasture, things sometimes happen to us in God's pasture. However, when an injury or illness happens to my horses, I take care of them as soon as I discover the issue. I provide the medicine that they need and daily wound care. Just like God promises to take care of us.

Meditating on God's boundaries and disciplining ourselves to stay within those boundaries brings peace during trials because through the chaos going on around us, we know that we are where we're supposed to be. We're still inside God's pasture, he will come to our aid.

I realized a second component to this, though. Most horses can become what's called "barn sour" or "buddy sour". "Barn sour" is when a horse refuses to leave the farm. When the owner takes the horse off the property, the horse needs to trust the rider's ability to keep her safe in the unknown. Until she has that assurance, her security is her pasture, her barn, her buddies, etc. Unless we trust God to take us off the property and into the unknown, we can become "barn sour", too. At least I know that I have. *So how do I apply this to my relationship with Goldie?* I wondered to myself. I knew that going back to the basics is always helpful because it's like a "reboot" for confidence. When you have a horse go back to doing something that they already know and they experience the rewards, it rebuilds their confidence in themselves and their rider. *How far back to the basics was I going to have to go?* I wondered to myself. "You're doing it right now," God said to me. I looked over and saw that as Goldie and I were walking together, she was very relaxed. We were walking together but were each on our sides of the small minimum maintenance road. The only thing attaching us was the lead rope, almost fully extended.

"You've given her nearly the whole rope of freedom. You are allowing her to walk as close or as far from you as she wants, but being responsible for her safety, you're holding onto a small part of the rope to maintain a level of control for her safety. She can enjoy a walk near you, knowing that she has some freedom while also knowing that she has the security of you being nearby." As I pondered over this, comparing it to how God relates to me, I felt a sharp tug on the lead rope. I panicked when I saw that my lack of attention caused the lead rope to drag too low and Goldie stepped on it. I cringed at the idea of her flashing back to the traumatic incident the other day, but she didn't. She just stopped and I quickly moved the lead rope away from her feet.

"See God, I'm an incompetent idiot."

"Is that what you saw from this?" God asked me. "Did you notice how Goldie immediately stopped when she stepped on the lead rope and calmly waited for you to move the lead rope? Then she waited for you to begin leading again?" God asked me. "Feeling the pressure on her nose, she remembered the pain the pressure from the rope halter caused her after fleeing from the ATVs. That response caused her to immediately stop. You're removing the rope from her feet reinforced to her that you can remove the stressful and painful rope, if she remains close to you and allows you to do so," God explained to me.

We finally got my tractor tires filled with gravel. These were a part of my training obstacle course. Positioned one in front of the other, with the largest one in the middle and filling them with gravel, created a way for me to ride up them similar to climbing a mountain. I was so excited to finally get to use them.

I figured the best way to go back to the basics was to go back to the obstacle course. We needed to go back to what we knew we were capable of, in order to remind us of the trust that we had. Additionally, I needed to add new obstacles so that we could grow in our confidence of one another by facing new challenges. The beauty of an obstacle course is that it is done in the safety of your property. I hand walked Goldie through the course first. She was very pushy but compliant. Then I mounted her to ride her through the course. We successfully made it up and over the tractor tire mountain from one direction, but we weren't successful in making it up and over from the other direction. The more that I pushed her to keep trying, the more frustrated she became. I realized that if I didn't stop while we were ahead, even our obstacle course work would create a breakdown of our relationship. So, I got off of her and simply hand walked her through the course again, then called it a night.

A few days later, I woke up intending to ride Goldie up the road. I decided that I was going to see how she was doing and plan accordingly, but that was my pie in the sky goal. I got her out of the pasture and walked her over to my mounting barrel. Most people use a mounting "block", but I use whatever is most handy, which at the moment is a plastic barrel cut in half. Goldie was calm and quiet, so I mounted her. She stood quietly so I just took some time to deep breath and relax. I had let her get away from this critical step, recently. Most of the time, it was because Tony would already be on Blaze and so I'd want to get going right away. Recently it was because Goldie would get danc-y pranc-y with me, and instead of taking the time to correct her, I'd just start riding her right away and redirect her while riding. I noticed that by just sitting and deep breathing, it was like we were calibrating our minds and energy into calmness. I had her stand for a few minutes as I just worked on deep breathing and enjoying inhaling peace and calm. I then began riding out the driveway. We made it to the neighbor's house where she once again locked up. However, this time, I was able to give her little squeezes and she complied and stepped forward. Immediately, I removed my legs from her sides to reward her effort. We had to do this a few more times, but she continued to comply easily each time. This was huge! I was praising God and telling Goldie how proud I was of her. She even relaxed enough to where I was able to take some pictures.

I began talking to God, "Please God, I know that confidence comes from overcoming scary situations, but I think that because this is our first ride since the incident…well, I just think that a scary situation would be too much for us, and might wreck us worse. I know that I don't know everything, and I shouldn't be trying to advise you on what's best for us, so whatever you think is best…but I'd like it if you could just send your angels to guard us and keep us safe. We need a good ride to start bringing us back our confidence."

The next thing I knew, I had dropped my phone. I couldn't believe it. The first thing I said to myself was, *Well, that serves you right. You should've known better than to be playing with your phone. You're not very responsible. This is your first ride out on Goldie and you're gonna play on your phone? What were you thinking? It's no wonder that you have so many problems, you never pay attention. You never think.*

I'm confident that I'm not the only one who repeats messages such as these to themselves. What about you? Do you ever struggle with negative self-talk? Hang on, friend, I have some encouragement for you. It was in this situation that God spoke truth to me, helping to reshape my thought processing and changed my life.

I stopped chewing myself out, dismounted and picked up my phone. Goldie was still standing calmly. We continued walking to the minimum maintenance road, but immediately as we got onto the minimum maintenance road, there was a vehicle approaching from behind. I knew there was very little threat of the vehicle coming down the road, so I kept walking, but Goldie started to panic. The vehicle continued to get louder as it drew closer. It was a dump truck style truck. He wasn't coming down the minimum maintenance road but Goldie didn't know that. She tossed her head and immediately began pulling back and backing up away from me. This was exactly the scene that unfolded with the ATVs. She reached the end of the lead rope and panicked again, rearing and bolting forward. She wasn't listening to me. She couldn't. She didn't hear me or see me. She was in panic mode. I held the lead rope firmly and tried to get her to lunge in a circle. She tried charging past me. I was surprised to notice that I had supernatural calm within me. I just kept breathing calmly and speaking low and soft, trying to get her to move in a circle. "It's ok, baby. You're fine. Come on, now. It'll be ok." She started to calm down and I saw that she was back to focusing on me, but she was still terrified. I began chewing myself out again for my failure as a responsible capable leader.

Then I felt in my spirit that God was telling me that dropping my phone wasn't MY MISTAKE, rather, he allowed me to drop my phone because he knew ahead of time that that truck was coming, and he knew what was going to happen. He protected us from a really bad wreck and further damage to our relationship. He answered my prayer for safety! He didn't answer in the way that I had asked; I asked him to protect me from any stressful situation because, in my limited perspective, I didn't think our relationship could withstand any more stress. I was afraid of stressful situations because I didn't believe that I could properly handle the situation and thus continue eroding the trust that Goldie had in me. He allowed what appeared to be my mistake to protect us from a really bad accident as a result of Goldie's panic! I began thanking him and praising him. Then my mind immediately began replaying the situation, trying to visualize how I would've handled it if I had been riding. What would I have done to stay on and work her through it? My approach in life was to control as much of my environment, to make it as stress-free as possible so that I was emotionally and mentally able to function appropriately. However, God was teaching me something new.

Then I heard God speak to me, "Kiddo, it's not always about preventing something from happening. It's about trusting that I'm already ahead of you and in control. You need to learn to relax and just roll with whatever life throws at you, trusting me for the outcome."

I started crying because that is how I live my life; always trying to plan, always trying to prevent bad things from happening. You know the old saying, "An ounce of prevention is worth a pound of cure". That's how I lived my life. Maybe you know what I'm talking about.

Truth be told, it is a burdensome way to live. My mind never shuts off because I'm always analyzing all the potential scenarios and all the plans of how I'll deal with all of the potential scenarios. Always blaming myself for every bad thing that happens, believing it's because I failed in some way. I think this thought pattern has come from years of constant criticism from those who held power over me. Throughout my past, I learned that to avoid being yelled at, ridiculed, shamed and or physically punished, I had to always make the right choice. Never making mistakes. To avoid these consequences, I had to strive for perfection. Even in times of trying to seek professional help, I received criticism by the professionals in the presence of my children which once again shamed me and even undermined my authority as a parent. Professionals mean well, that is why they get into the career, to begin with, but they are human and prone to human error and human error no matter how well the intentions, can still be damaging.

Those messages from others became my personal messages. Without being conscious of this, perfection then became the standard that I held for myself throughout my life. My perfectionism wasn't driven from the motive to be "better than anyone else" per se, it was driven from the motive of avoiding punishment and suffering consequences and to feel that I was "acceptable".

It is strange to me, because throughout the years that my children were growing up, my mantra in our home was, "progress, -not perfection". I never wanted my children to know the pressure of having to strive for perfection, instead, I wanted them to focus on progress. I was intentional about stressing that "progress" is measured differently for each person and that any progress, no matter how small it looked, was still progress. However, looking back, I can see that even stressing the importance of continued progress may have been a branch from the weed of perfectionism. I see evidence of how my struggles with perfectionism still impacted my children. I see how I tried to prevent them from taking risks. In my mind, it was all about protecting them from the consequences. I didn't realize it at the time, but I believe that my neuroticism was suffocating my children. Instead of depending on God's guidance on how to raise my children, I was relying on my instincts and intellect and the overwhelming advice from others. In a sense, I was once again trying to be God. Now, granted, as a parent, it is our responsibility to protect our children from potential harm, but I've since realized that there are times where we need to allow our kids to take age-appropriate risks, teaching them how to weight the pros and the cons and then allowing them the freedom to take that risk. It's teaching them how to live courageously in an exhilarating, adventurous life. Doing anything worthwhile that holds eternal value is going to require courage.

How difficult a job we parents have! If you are a parent, I can only encourage you, dear friend to seek God's guidance and give yourself grace and give others grace.

Walking along the trail with Goldie, I remembered a conversation that I'd had with Tony about the stress that I was under at the time. I remembered telling him how I had spent years learning about myself and learning about how to handle my emotions. I learned my emotional triggers for my anxiety, depression and stress. I knew where my thresholds were and knew what I needed to do to take care of myself before reaching those thresholds to be able to function at my best. I remember expressing my frustration to Tony because the current demands on my life prevented me from taking care of myself and pushed me beyond my thresholds. I was angry because I felt like I was being denied the ability to take care of my mental health.

It was at this moment that I realized that maybe God was bringing me to a new place. It's no longer about me controlling the environments that I find myself in, or guarding a perceived threshold and managing my emotions through coping techniques. Maybe God is telling me that He's removing my thresholds entirely and complete reliance on His strength is all that is required.

I began walking Goldie again and saw how calm she had gotten. God spoke to me and told me once again, how I'm so much like Goldie. Goldie loves me, she respects me, and yes, she trusts me to a certain point. When she feels terrified self-preservation trumps trust in me. I'm a lot like that in my relationship with God. I asked God, "So, how do I increase her trust in me?" God said to me, "Well, you're doing it right now. She was terrified, but by managing your energy, you helped her to calm down. You showed her that you can be relied upon to be her source of peace and calm. Then, instead of pushing her to get over her fear and getting back on her, you chose to just walk alongside her. You let her decompress and process what just happened and simply walked alongside her. Isn't that how I work with you?"

I looked over at Goldie, walking alongside me. Her head was lowered and relaxed. Her ears were forward and her pace was gentle. She was so observant of my every move that I could direct her with my own pace or simply by moving my hand over into her space. It was so strange to me, how tight of a bond her and I have when she's calm, yet when she panics, she becomes dangerous because she isn't able to see me, hear me, or think clearly.

I took Goldie out for a ride about a month or so later with my son, Tim, walking alongside us. We went around the square. It was a wonderfully relaxing ride until we were on the home stretch. We were passing the neighbor's house when I heard one of their 5 Rottweilers barking and running out to the road. Goldie got nervous, and to be honest, I was nervous, too. The neighbor's dogs are nice dogs, however, a person never knows how a dog will react if they perceive a threat to their home. Instinctively and without hesitation, I turned Goldie around, facing her towards the Rottweiler and encouraged her to walk towards the dog. I shouted at the dog to go back to his home. Tim also walked towards the dog and talking in a loud voice, commanded the dog to go back home. I was proud of Goldie and myself for being calm, confident and assertive. I resisted the urge to ponder what I would've done had the whole pack met us at the road.

I felt a stirring in my spirit--faint as a light breeze whispering through the leaves in the towering trees. I felt something rising within myself: fear being replaced with courage. Not from gaining knowledge or from using logic or from having a sealed tight plan. God is transforming me. As my heart desires to grow, it's as though I can sense him paring away all of the layers of self-preservation that I've relied on, and replacing it with layers of courage built from faith and trust in him.

As I said before, I believe that fear is the biggest barrier to loving others and doing good to others. Our fear of rejection keeps us from opening our hearts to others. Fear of getting hurt keeps us from loving others fully and with our whole hearts. Fear of others getting something that we want keeps us from giving what we have. Where are you, friend? Do you have fears that are preventing you from experiencing true, deep love and joy? God wants to envelop you in his love and drive out that fear so that you can live a courageous life of bold love.

I am reminded of a saying, "we are human beings, not human doings." We glorify God by being who he created us to be. We don't have to be consumed with trying to do what we think he wants us to do. We can just be who he created us to be. All of creation glorifies God by simply being what he created it to be.

Psalm 19:1 states, "The heavens declare the glory of God; the skies proclaim the work of his hands." Psalm 96:11-12 states, "Let the heavens rejoice, let the earth be glad; let the sea resound, and all that is in it. Let the fields be jubilant, and everything in them, let all the trees of the forest sing for joy." Job 12:7-8 says, "But ask the animals and they will teach you, or the birds in the sky and they will tell you; or speak to the earth, and it will teach you, or let the fish in the sea inform you."

When we consider nature and the beauty and joy that it brings us, aren't we moved to marvel at the goodness of God? Perhaps this is all the "good deeds" that God requires of us. That we allow Him to transform us into the beings that He intended us to be, so that simply by our existence; simply by being who we are, people will consider the beauty, the love and the joy that we bring the world and then they will be moved to marvel at the goodness of God.

Chapter 19

Whose Plans Prevail?

Commit to the Lord whatever you do and He will establish your plans. —**Proverbs 16:3**

How are you feeling about the direction of your life? Are you in a place where you feel content that you've accomplished everything that you've wanted to? Or do you have more goals and dreams that you're hoping to realize?

In my early 40's, and with all of my children being adults themselves, I had great plans for the rest of my life. My heart was yearning for adventures now that my children were all grown. I had this crazy dream of riding across Minnesota. Honestly, I've had this fantasy for about a couple of decades of being a type of circuit rider. A person who travels on horseback sharing the gospel of Jesus. I had read many stories of brave women (many of which were at least in their 40's, some even well into their 60's) who had ridden across the United States of America, and although I knew that I would never accomplish a feat such as that, I felt that riding across Minnesota was more achievable.

I knew that my horses needed to be properly conditioned for a task such as that. The farthest that I had ridden Goldie in one day was about 14 miles. I researched conditioning schedules and joined an online horse group for motivation, tips, encouragement and accountability.

On January 1, 2020, I felt a new sense of determination and motivation. I truly believed that this was going to be my year. My goal was working on getting the horses properly conditioned and begin my trek across MN in June 2022. I had my plan and goals all mapped out. The training days and the skills we would work on were all written down in my planner. This was gonna be our year of no more excuses. I would discipline myself and maximize all of my free time in training.

As has always been the case in my life, circumstances once again got in my way. The biggest challenge was COVID-19. All "non-essential" businesses were forced to close down. This included "non-essential" vet care. I had our vet and an equine chiropractor lined up to come out and get us riding ready for the 2020 season, but it all had to be put on hold. Additionally, my windows of opportunities for working with the horses were very small, because

Jenna and Rose were living with us. Jenna had been working for a home care company helping elderly people with homemaking skills so that they can stay in their homes. She also began working on her Certified Nursing Assistant license to make her more employable and increase her level of pay. So, when I wasn't at work myself, most days I was also babysitting Rose.

I decided to discipline myself to get up early in the mornings before anyone else was awake to have my time with the horses. Getting up at 5:30 am made for very long days, especially on those days that Jenna worked until 9 pm.

As life with COVID-19 started to calm down, the governor began loosening up his restrictions, and we were able to get the equine chiropractor to come out and work on Goldie and Blaze. She recommended shoes for Goldie, so we called our farrier, Kim and set up an appointment with her. Around this same time, I began noticing that Blaze was walking around less and laying down more frequently and for long periods. He displayed similar behavior last year and one of our vets suggested putting shoes on him. Once we did that, he seemed immediately better. So, I contacted Kim and told her that I'd like for her to put shoes on Blaze as well.

Then one day, I was outside and I noticed him trying to get up from laying down. It broke my heart to see him struggling with trying to get up. I could tell by how long it took him to stand, and by the way, he moved that he was in pain. I couldn't understand why the shoes weren't helping him like they had last year. Suspecting laminitis, I spoke with Tony about it and told him that we have to pull Blaze off the grass and feed him only hay. We had just replaced the engine in the truck that I use to deliver mail, so we really couldn't afford a vet to come out and look at him at this time. I called Kim and asked her for her advice. She stated that for as long as she's been working on our horses' hooves, she never saw evidence of laminitis. I prayed, "God, please help us. We can't afford a vet. Please give us the wisdom and the knowledge to know how to help Blaze and please use Kim to help us fix his feet. And Lord, if you're willing, I'd sure like it if you'd just heal his feet."

We built another fence line, creating a division so that all the horses were restricted to a rectangular area with the lean-to and water tank. I figured it wouldn't hurt any of them to stay off the grass and only on hay, at least until Kim could get here and take care of Blaze's feet. Although he continued to show signs of being in pain, there were visible signs of the pain becoming less severe.

One day, while Tony and I were cleaning the garage, I noticed some pool noodles, and I had this idea of cutting the pool noodles into horseshoe shapes and using them as cushions for Blaze's feet. I told Tony my idea and looking around in the garage, he found some large squares of packing foam and he cut rectangles out of it. Using vet wrap, we fastened the foam padding onto his feet. Miraculously, the next day, he showed virtually no signs of pain! We praised God for giving us the idea, and called Kim, asking her if she could put shoes on Blaze that also contained padding. She said yes, she could and she would do that when she came the following week.

During this same time was the incident that occurred with the ATVs and Goldie bolting, resulting in damaged trust between her and me. To be honest, I was discouraged, to say the least. Our society says that you can achieve whatever you put your mind to. With enough hard work and dedication, you can do anything. The sky's the limit for those who are disciplined and diligent, right?

I was frustrated and angry because it seemed like no matter what I did, no matter how hard I tried, I just couldn't arrange my life in a way that would enable me to reach my goals.

One day in my online horse group, the instructor had a class on breaking down the barriers that get in the way of reaching our goals. She also provided a worksheet for us to download that we were to use to identify our goals, identify our barriers and identify the steps that we could take to start breaking down the barriers. I did a worksheet on each of our horses. My goal for Goldie was to rebuild our trust and confidence so that I could ride her independently around the square again. My goal for Blaze was to get his feet healed so that he could ride around the square again. My goal for Faith was to get her emotionally secure enough to be a good pony for our granddaughter, Rose. Lastly, my goal for Hope was to get her trained to ride.

To be honest, the day that I wrote those goals, I didn't know if I could reach them. I believed that it would take a lot of time, consistency, and money, none of which was in large supply for us. But I decided to just start. I decided that the one thing that was for certain was that no progress would be made at all if I didn't do something. I decided that I would just do what I could with the time that I had. As the old saying goes, "Inch by inch...it's a cinch!".[2]

I began by just hand walking Goldie around the square. Then I added riding part of the way and hand walking part of the way. With Faith, I started with just grooming her, then lunging her. As she grew proficient in lunging, I started saddling her after being lunged and then taking the saddle off. When she showed no anxiety at being saddled, then I began lunging her with the saddle on. With Hope, I worked on lunging and hand walking through the

---

[2] For non-horse savvy people, this is a play on words. The cinch is attached to one side of the saddle and goes under the belly and fastens to the other side of the saddle. Kinda like a belt for a horse.

obstacle course. With Blaze, I focused on just keeping his feet comfortable.

One day as I was lunging Faith with the saddle on, and noticing the calm in her, I prayed for wisdom from God. I asked him if I should take her to the next level. Feeling peace, I asked Tony to bring Rose over. I told him my idea. He and I used to volunteer with a therapeutic riding organization serving individuals with disabilities. One person led the horse, while one or two people walked alongside, offering support to the rider. I asked him to do the same for Rose. We would put Rose in the saddle, I would lead Faith, and Tony would walk alongside holding Rose so that if Faith spooked, he would just lift Rose off. Faith is a little Shetland pony and Tony and I both tower over her, so I had no concerns about safety doing it this way.

My heart still swells with joy as I look at the pictures that Tim got of the moment. Rose was gripping the horn with both hands and she had the biggest grin across her face. She truly is a horse girl! Tony said that she kept pushing his hands off of her because she didn't want him holding her. Faith did beautifully. No problems whatsoever. Her confidence and curiosity continue to grow to the point that she is beginning to initiate relationship while in the pasture! I could not believe the transformation that had taken place within her.

The most recent display of transformation within Faith is a moment when Rose wanted to ride Faith. I had Faith out in the yard, just working on groundwork. Rose wanted to come over to us, so I let her pet Faith. Then she started crying and motioning "up" with her arms. I knew that she wanted to ride, but I didn't have her saddle on. Jenna and Tony came over because they were going to help me give Rose a ride on Faith bareback. Rose was crying loudly and I told Tony that I was not going to allow Rose to ride Faith if she was going to continue carrying on like that. I didn't feel it was fair to Faith to have to listen to all that and still be expected to remain calm. However, I watched Faith standing there so quietly and patiently. She even turned to look at Rose almost as if she was saying, "Hey. What's the matter, kid?" Rose quieted down and then Tony lifted her onto Faith's back and we walked around in a few circles before I decided that Faith did enough and could go back to her herd.

The relationship between Goldie and I is restored to where she and I are riding around the square independently again. We even had an experience of a dirt biker passing us. Although Goldie was terrified (so was I) she trusted me enough to help her work through it without me having to dismount!

I can ride Hope in our training pasture, navigating around the barrels, weaving in and out of the poles. We have practiced riding over the mattress and up and down the tractor tire mountain. Our most recent success is riding a short distance up our gravel road (with Blaze by her side).

I found some hoof supplements for Blaze, that had a lot of positive reviews. His feet are improving enough to where he is back to running around the pasture and Tony and I were even able to do several rides together around the square recently.

I was marveling at all of these successes one day and realized that these were achieved despite the lack of time for consistent training. I just did what I could with the time that I had. God provided the increase. Proverbs 16:9 states, "In their hearts, humans plan their course, but the Lord establishes their steps."

These successes were experienced proofs that I don't have to stress and micromanage every spare minute of every day to accomplish things. I love Psalm 20:4. It states, "May he give you the desire of your heart and make all your plans succeed.". What I gained from these experiences is the freedom to be able to ask God every day, "Lord, what is important today?" I am free to focus my energies on what he tells me is important for the day, and I can trust him to work out the things that are important to me, but don't necessarily have the time to make a priority.

To be honest, I don't know if it's God will to help me accomplish all the desires of my heart, but I've come to a place of genuine contentment about that. Maybe he will, but maybe it won't be with Goldie and Blaze. Goldie is 15 years old this year and Blaze is 14. None of us is equipped for strenuous, challenging rides anymore. Maybe for this season, Goldie and Blaze have the purpose of being my best friends and they'll be great teachers for Rose and the other grandkids. Maybe for my crazy adventures, God has different horses picked out for me when that time comes. Maybe that time won't ever come this side of eternity. It's okay. I'm reaching a place of peace. God is working in my heart, showing me the things that are so much more important than my dreams for adventure.

He continues to show me that everything that I learn through these wonderful horses is molding me into a new person. I get to share who I am and what I know with my children and grandchildren, hopefully leaving with them bits and pieces of myself contributing to parts of who they are. That's how you leave a legacy. And that is so much bigger and amazing than any dream I could have for myself. God truly is great and big and amazing. He takes our dreams and exchanges them for even bigger dreams that are beyond our understanding and comprehension. He speaks to us as he spoke to Jeremiah in Jeremiah 29:11, "For I know the plans I have for you", declares the Lord. "Plans to prosper you and not to harm you, plans to give you hope and a future."

Friend, you can trust God with your dreams. If you hand your dreams over to him, I guarantee that he'll help you achieve so much more than you can even imagine.

Lean forward and give a squeeze. Hang onto your hat, 'cause we're on the home stretch.

Chapter 20

You scratch My Back, I Scratch Yours

Do unto others as you would have them do unto you. —Luke 6:31

One of the neatest things that I've witnessed with my horses is watching them groom each other. Two of them will stand facing one another and using their teeth, they'll scratch each other's backs and or necks.

My Goldie loves being scratched so much that she will walk up to me in the pasture and position her body next to mine in the exact place where she wants to be scratched. If I miss the mark, she'll move forward or backwards to guide me where she wants to be scratched. She is lead mare so she doesn't let anyone else receive any scratches from me until she's gotten scratched and is satisfied, herself.

Another neat thing that I've observed is when one or more of them are laying down, the others are standing watch over the ones lying down. With all the beauty of the herd, a troublesome thing about the bond of the herd is that when one leaf, say with me on a short little ride, they all get worried and will run the fence line, crying out incessantly, to whoever is with me. They are devoted to one another and look out for one another.

Being misunderstood by other people has given me a greater sensitivity in trying to understand others, myself. Although I am a born again Christian, I'm still an imperfect human being and I am a work in progress. I have offended people without meaning to, and people have cast judgement about me based on those incidences. I wish people understood me better and understood my heart. I am kind and compassionate, but there are times when I say something stupid or insensitive. There are even times when I'm careless with my words. I don't mean to, but in my human-ness, it does happen at times. I'm sure that you understand what I'm talking about.

What I've learned from those experiences is to try to be patient and understanding of other people. I try to see things from their perspective to try to understand why they might be speaking or acting a certain way. If I know the person is a believer, I try to consider that maybe this is just an area in which they're still growing in. Don't get me wrong. I am not perfect. There are days where I am exhausted from the demands and I get crabby. Then I can become cynical, critical, impatient and judgmental of others. Fortunately, God convicts me quickly and I'm able to apologize to him and set my mind on being more understanding of others. Even this action is a gift of humility from God. As I see my imperfection and need for grace, it shows me that others are imperfect and in need of grace. In all honesty, being a believer in Jesus is incredibly difficult and incredibly simple all at the same time. On the one hand, it's incredibly simple in the sense that Jesus is the one who does all of the work in us. Jesus states in John 15:5, "I am the vine; you are the branches. If you remain in me and I in you, you will bear much fruit; apart from me you can do nothing." On the other hand, it's incredibly difficult, because it requires us to be able to see with honesty the areas that we are struggling in, then we have to agree with Jesus that changes need to be made, then we have to yield to the Spirit every time we're tempted in that area. That in itself is very difficult at first because it goes against our nature. We function a certain way for so long that it is a part of who we are, our personality.

We need to be able to allow ourselves grace in the growth process, but we also need to be able to allow others grace as they grow. Additionally, we need to leave their growth between them and God. Romans 14:4 states, "Who are you to judge someone else's servant? To their own master, servants stand or fall. And they will stand, for the Lord can make them stand." Our job is to love them as they are and believe in them and the future person that God will transform them into.

The verses preceding and following Luke 6:31 present greater challenges. They discuss loving one's enemies. Luke 6:27-28 states, "But I tell you who hear me: Love your enemies, do good to those who hate you, bless those who curse you, pray for those who mistreat you." Verse 35 states, "But love your enemies, do good to them, and lend to them without expecting to get anything back."

One of the most difficult things that I've had to learn to do is to love people who have deeply wounded my children. For some of these people, I'm still working through my emotions of anger and hurt and have to consciously choose to forgive them in my mind every time the thought pops into my head. For others, I constantly bounce back and forth between anger and empathy as I understand their background and why they made the choices they made. Still, there are others that God has given me the ability to truly forgive and genuinely love. I'm so thankful that God is patient with us as he helps us work through these things.

What about you, friend? Is there someone that you're struggling to forgive and offer Christ-like love to? Trust me, forgiving someone is as good for your own heart as it is for the person you're forgiving. Maybe more so. Hanging onto anger and bitterness poisons your own soul. Forgiving someone of a wrong committed against you isn't excusing it, but it's releasing the negative emotions and desire for revenge into the hands of a just God.

1 Corinthians 13 is considered "the Love" chapter. It explains what love is and what it isn't. Verses 1-3 states, "If I speak in the tongues of men and of angels, but have not love, I am only a resounding gong or a clanging cymbal. If I have the gift of prophecy and can fathom all mysteries and all knowledge, and if I have a faith that can move mountains, but have not love, I am nothing. If I give all I possess to the poor and surrender my body to the flames, but have not love, I gain nothing." What Paul is saying here, is that my Christian gifts, talents, abilities, and virtues are practically worthless if I'm not using them to love others.

Verses 4-8 state, "Love is patient, love is kind. It does not envy, it does not boast, it is not proud. It is not rude, it is not self-seeking, it is not easily angered, it keeps no record of wrongs. Love does not delight in evil but rejoices with the truth. It always protects, always trusts, always hopes, always perseveres. Love never fails." These verses tell us what love does and doesn't look like. These are tall orders in close relationships, how much more difficult in relationships with people we consider as our enemies.

Praise God, that through the Spirit's help, we can genuinely love others. Galatians 5:22-25 states, "But the fruit of the Spirit is love, joy, peace, patience, kindness, goodness, faithfulness, gentleness, and self-control. Against such things, there is no law. Those who belong to Christ Jesus have crucified the sinful nature with its passions and desires. Since we live by the Spirit, let us keep in step with the Spirit." What Paul is saying here is that if we have given our lives to Jesus, we need to be serious about living as he did, being willing to "crucify" or take drastic measures to kill the sinful desires within us. In choosing to deny our sinful natures and choosing to rely on the Spirit, the Spirit himself grows his fruit (as mentioned above) within us. He gives us the ability to love others--even our enemies.

An even harder battle in my mind has been over the atrocities committed on innocent children. Ending child abuse and sex trafficking have been causes that I'm passionate about. I've struggled with knowing how to handle my thoughts and emotions in regards to the abusers of these children. How do I see these people through God's eyes? How can I love them? If I'm required to love them, how do I do that while advocating for the victims? What is the best way to deal with people who do such evil things?

God spoke to me and told me that I need to change my focus. My focus can't be on trying to eradicate evil to prevent evil things from happening but to help those who have experienced the evil things. That gave me a tremendous amount of peace. James 1:27 states, "Religion that God our Father accepts as pure and faultless is this: to look after orphans and widows in their distress and to keep oneself from being polluted by the world." I don't know how many of the children who are victims of trafficking are orphans, but I believe the principle here is that God wants us to look after those who are most vulnerable in our society. Which includes all children regardless of whether they're truly orphans or not.

Additionally, I cannot express how much peace I've gained from taking my husband's advice (which I believe aligns with the second half of what James is saying in James 1:27). Tony's motto is a fishing analogy. He says, "keep your eye on your own bobber", when advising people to mind their own business. Or as a current philosophy goes, "You do you and let me do me." Don't hear me wrong. I don't believe in moral relativism. I believe that there is Absolute Truth, and that comes from God in the person of Jesus. Jesus said, "I am the way and the truth and the life." (John 14:6.). However, I believe that God wants us to focus his Truth on ourselves. His Word should be the ruler we use to measure our own walk, not to be used to measure someone else's. That is how we will ensure that we are keeping ourselves from being polluted by the world. We are told to confront sin in other people, but only in love and only with love as the motive, and I would say that we need to hear directly from God about when and how to confront another person's sin.

It was several weeks later that God went deeper with me in explaining this to me with the following Scriptures:

> **Say to those with fearful hearts, 'Be strong, do not fear; your God will come, he will come with vengeance; with divine retribution he will come to save you.' Then will the eyes of the blind be opened and the ears of the deaf unstopped. Then will the lame leap like a deer, and the mute tongue shout for joy. Water will gush forth in the wilderness and streams in the desert. —Isaiah 35:4-6**

> **The blind receive sight, the lame walk, those who have leprosy are cleansed, the deaf hear, the dead are raised and the good news is proclaimed to the poor. —Matthew 11:5.**

God pointed out to me that because he is also just, I don't have to worry, because he will deal with evil. However, he is the one to deal with it; not me. Galatians 6:7-9 states, "Do not be deceived: God cannot be mocked. A man reaps what he sows. Whoever sows to please their flesh, from the flesh will reap destruction; whoever sows to please the Spirit, from the Spirit will reap eternal life. Let us not become weary in doing good, for at the proper time we will reap a harvest if we do not give up."

When Jesus came to earth some 2000 years ago, he came in love, compassion, mercy and grace. He came to provide for our physical needs as well as our spiritual needs. God brought to my attention that nowhere in the Gospels did it mention anything about Jesus using his authority to punish people. He warned them, but he didn't punish them.

When Jesus was teaching in the synagogue in Nazareth, he read from the scroll of Isaiah, quoting, "The Spirit of the Lord is on me, because he has anointed me to proclaim good news to the poor. He has sent me to proclaim freedom for the prisoners and recovery of sight for the blind, to set the oppressed free, to proclaim the year of the Lord's favor." Then he rolled up the scroll, gave it back to the attendant and sat down." Luke 4:16-20. When we look at the Scripture that he was quoting from (Isaiah 61). we see that he stopped reading and sat down without also reading "and the day of vengeance of our God."

Essentially, he put a period where Isaiah had a comma. Jesus was informing them (and us) that his first coming was a mission of love, mercy and grace. He first came as our kinsman redeemer. Purchasing our freedom with his blood. When he returns the second time, he will come as the avenger of blood. There will be a day when God will judge the world. Those who haven't accepted Jesus' sacrifice for their sins, will be judged and condemned for their sins.

For now, we are in the age of grace. God spoke to me and told me that this is also my mission. My mission is not to be preoccupied with how to handle injustice. My mission is to care for those treated unjustly. By taking my focus off of trying to handle injustice, I'm no longer focusing on the people committing the injustices. It has allowed me to see them as hurt people doing hurtful things.

Day by day God finds ways to remind me of my brokenness and the hurt that I have done to people in my brokenness to fill me with compassion for others who also cause hurt to others. My mission needs to be that of Jesus'. Helping meet felt physical needs and helping point people to Jesus who can meet their spiritual needs.

That's not to say that there's no place for justice. We need an earthly justice system. God instituted an earthly justice system because he knew the importance of restitution and retribution, and he also understood that left up to us, we'd misuse our legal and justice systems. An interesting perspective that I was presented with regarding God's mandate in Exodus 21:24 and Leviticus 24:20 for "eye for an eye and tooth for a tooth" is that it was not necessarily meant to be viewed only from the perspective of "I can do to you exactly what you did to me" rather also from the perspective of "I'm only allowed to do to you just what you've done to me -nothing more-". It was a way for the wronged person to receive justice, while also being just to the person who did wrong. I am persuaded to believe this view because I think we as humans have a tendency to act rashly and from our emotions when hurt and seeking "justice". As James 1:20 states, "Human anger does not bring about the righteousness of God."

Jesus tells us in John 13:34-35, "A new command I give you: Love one another. As I have loved you, so you must love one another. By this everyone will know that you are my disciples, if you love one another." By following Jesus' example, and doing unto others what we would have them do unto us, we are in fact, loving our neighbor as ourselves. Like my little herd of horses, we'll have the security of bonded relationships where each member looks out for the others.

Chapter 21

The Truth Hurts...Or Helps

As iron sharpens iron, so one person sharpens another. —Proverbs 27:17

Pastor Bruce's sermon was about "What makes an effective Christian Witness"?

He noted some points as follows:

1. Effective Christian witnesses are "Cross-Centered": They keep their eyes on Jesus' completed work for themselves and others at the cross.

2. Effective Christian witnesses are focused: They don't get sidetracked.

3. They are "Backyard Bold" and are intentional within their own spheres of influence.

4. They are storytellers: they love sharing their conversion stories.

5. They are Holy Spirit powered: Completely reliant on the Spirit's power, believing that with God all things are possible.

I also made some personal notes that they are "salt" to the world. Through sharing the Gospel message, they are spiritual "preservatives". Additionally, salt adds flavor, but we have to be careful that our flavor isn't overpowering or bitter.

I felt my heart quicken with renewed excitement and hope. You see, lately, I have been struggling a lot with feeling like my brain is cluttered. It seems that my life is so chaotic, that my brain resembles my life. There's so much going on at the same time, or at least in rapid succession, that I don't feel like I have even time to think. I simply react; moving from one expectation to the next. I feel like I'm doing so many things, but I wonder how much of it has any real value. I struggle with the questions, *Am I doing the right things with my life right now? "Should I be doing something else? What am I supposed to be doing?* I've been learning so much about myself from the sermons preached at church and through Christian literature, but I don't have the time to process what I'm learning. On the other hand, do I need to process and understand everything to still be effective? Does anyone else feel completely confused and inadequate? I'm so thankful for my "Legacy Church" family. We have a beautiful family where we are allowed to be real. People are willing to listen to your hurts and they're willing to share their hurts with you so that you don't feel alone. Pastor Diane (Pastor Bruce's wife) is a dear friend and she prayed with me that God would help me sort out the chaos in my mind and that he would give me an extra special blessing today.

I knew that God was speaking to me through the sermon, but I needed to get home and go for a ride and listen for God to explain things to me. My mind is always clearest and I tend to hear God most clearly when I'm out riding in the woods.

My heart was hungering for adventure. It wasn't simply itching for something exciting. I felt in my spirit that I needed to do something daring. Like God was calling me out of my comfort zone into doing something that scared me. I've felt this for a while, but here I am, rationalizing all the reasons why I shouldn't take risks. That's what a responsible adult does, right? I noticed the parallel in my spiritual walk. How did I get here? What happened? After I surrendered my life to Jesus, I was on fire with the Holy Spirit. There was nothing he asked me to do, nowhere he asked me to go, that I didn't do or go. Life was an exhilarating adventure. I was brave and bold. What happened to me? Why have I gotten to the point of "playing it safe"? I realized that I lost my nerve in riding, way back when I got thrown off a few too many times. I realized that I lost my bold faith way back when life threw me off a few too many times.

Yet, here I was, this day, feeling like God was drawing me out. Beckoning me to do something daring. What should I do? I thought about loading Goldie into the trailer and taking her to the state forest nearby. It's been a long time since I was there, and it's so beautiful there! But…there's no cell phone service. If anything happened to me, I'd have no way of getting help. Besides, I don't even know how Goldie feels about a daring adventure.

Once back home, Tim helped me get Goldie out. I told him that I planned to ride Goldie around the square, but that I might ride her out into the county land if I think she's up for it. I didn't know how the ride was going to go, and to be honest, I was nervous about going out into the county land alone. We had just had a lot of rain, so I anticipated a lot of flooding and a lot of bugs. I didn't know how Goldie would handle it, and I didn't want to risk falling off without anyone to help me.

I rode Goldie down the gravel road and onto the minimum maintenance road, playing worship music and worshiping God as we went. As I stared down at the crossroad, God said to me, "Come to me out into the county land." Instead of taking our usual route to the left, I pointed Goldie straight ahead. She took a few steps, but seeing the huge water puddle, she snorted and tried turning towards the left. I gently said to her, "Come on, Goldie. God called us out here, so we gotta go. Besides, the water isn't that deep." I couldn't believe what happened next. She willingly turned around and began walking down the trail onto county land.

I couldn't believe that we were really doing this. We were out there all on our own! The creek was rushing loudly and quickly due to all the rain we'd had. We encountered lots of large puddles on narrow trails with low over-hung branches. We also got lost, and Goldie got frustrated. I realized that we needed to turn around and as I did so, Goldie started getting pushy and began trotting back the way we'd come. This was not good because of how tight the trails were. I heard God say to me," This is what adventure looks like. It's hard, it's messy, and it can be perilous, especially if you don't know where you're going or what you're doing. Are you sure you really want this?"

Sensing that God wasn't just speaking of horse-y adventure but also spiritual adventure, I said "Yes, Lord, I do. But I don't know how to start." God spoke to me and said, "You just start right where you're at like you're doing right now. Instead of taking Goldie to a state forest trail today, you decided to just start in your neighborhood by going off the minimum maintenance road onto county land. Loving me and loving others starts the same way. When the time is right, I will provide what you need to move forward."

We got back to the open clearing that we'd passed and I realized that I either needed to find another offshoot trail or we'd have to head all the way back to the crossroad. I asked God, "Please show us the trail to get back home." We went a short distance and saw another trail that we'd missed earlier, so I turned Goldie down that trail. She was reluctant at first. She wanted to go back the way we'd come. We'd already been down that trail and she knew that it led us back to the minimum maintenance road.

I spoke gently to her, "Baby, we don't wanna go all the way back. It'll be longer then, and we'll have to go back through all that water and bugs. Let's just keep going and see where this comes out at."

She hesitated at first, then complied; but as she relaxed, the ride became more enjoyable. I couldn't believe the beauty surrounding us. We were on a trail amid dense woods. The trees were so tall and so thick that it blocked out much of the sunlight. It felt as though it were dusk even though it was only about 3 pm. I heard God speak to me, "This is what you've been missing out on by playing it safe. There's a lot of beauty that you've been missing out on by playing it safe." Then God brought to mind my family and he spoke to me saying, "This is your priority. But when the time is right, I'll provide all that you need to move forward."

The trail came out on the other end of the minimum maintenance road, a more residential area. Goldie became nervous at the sounds of lawnmowers and began stepping out more quickly. Then she got nervous. I looked behind us and saw a huge white van pulling a trailer. I rode her down into the ditch, but the ditch was a very steep, narrow ditch, and she started to panic. For our safety, I got down off of her and tried to calm her down. She began reacting similarly as she did when she got spooked by the ATVs. However, I was able to keep the reins in my hands and I spoke calmly to her. She was terrified -her eyes were wide-, but she was listening to me. I scratched her neck. Another truck drove by, pulling a boat. Again, she started trying to pull away from me, but I kept her reins in my hands and continued talking calmly to her and scratching her neck. She stayed with me. I walked her up out of the ditch and onto the road and began taking the reins off of the clips on her rope halter. Before I could attach one end to the bottom of her rope halter, another truck drove by so closely, that I could've reached out and touched it while holding Goldie. She tried pulling away from me, but again, she stayed with me. I attached one of the clips to the bottom of her halter and hand walked her the rest of the way home. I kept telling her how proud I was of her, and how brave she was. The ride didn't end the way that I wanted it to, but it ended the way it was supposed to. With both of us home safe. It makes me think about my life. There's been a lot of fun, there's been a lot of sorrow, there's been a lot of close calls, and I'm sure there'll be more, but I have the confidence, that the ride will end just as it's supposed to.

Of course, true to my nature, I replayed the scenario over in my head, wondering what I could've done differently, and what I should do differently in the future. I worried that if I continued to get down every time we encountered a vehicle on the road, Goldie would develop a conditioned response to her nervousness of me getting down. I was once again feeling overwhelmed and confused. I felt that I needed to visit the pastors of our church.

At Pastor Bruce's and Pastor Diane's home, I was talking with them about my confusion, fear and general feelings of being overwhelmed. Pastor Bruce said something that struck me. He said that fear of the future is fear from the past just flipped over on its back. He said that when we experience painful things in our past, we tend to live our lives through that lens. The decisions that we make are based on pain from the past and the fear of going through it again. We try to learn to do things differently to avoid repeating the mistakes of the past that caused us such pain. This in and of itself, isn't bad. Actually, this shows wisdom and growth. However, this becomes problematic when we become obsessive about trying to avoid making the same mistakes. Especially when the motivation comes from fear. When Pastor Bruce explained these things to me, I realized that I was allowing fear to cause me to play god in my life. Because of fear, and to avoid pain and suffering, I was obsessed with obtaining knowledge and wisdom to use to control my own life and my circumstances. I'm sure you've heard the saying, "knowledge is power." I didn't realize what was happening, because seeking knowledge and wisdom is a good thing. Growth, maturity, and learning from one's mistakes is a good thing. However, making it an idol, using it for my purposes, to avoid God's purposes was the problem. I honestly believe that my confusion and feelings of being overwhelmed were a consequence of trying to wield power that I'm not equipped to handle.

Taking risks, and growing in courage in my horse riding, is helping me in my relationship with God. I'm finding that I'm experiencing more peace when adversity arises. I'm finding that I'm becoming more able to patiently wait to see what God is going to do, instead of panic. I'm growing in courage to take steps that involve risk, and trust God for the outcome, instead of trying to control every circumstance in each step of my life.

Recently I had a life-changing experience where through different sources, the Holy Spirit brought me to a higher level of understanding of myself; who I thought I was and I who am.

From all the trauma that I've experienced in my life, I had developed the assumption that "anxious and depressed" was my nature. it is just who I was. I was viewing myself as I viewed my horses. They are horses and by nature, as prey animals, they flee from danger. I saw myself similarly. Sure, I knew what Paul wrote to Timothy in 2 Timothy 1:7, "For God did not give us a spirit of timidity, but a spirit of power, of love and of self-discipline." However, I wasn't claiming that verse over my life appropriately. I had been claiming that verse in weakness and desperation. The Holy Spirit showed me this is not a verse that I need to cling to for convincing me that I will hopefully, someday be given a spirit of power. This spirit has already been given to me. I already have the Spirit of power, love and self-discipline!

I have to train my horses to trust me, and their courage comes from trusting me. I was assuming that the same applied to me and my relationship with God. I was assuming that with enough of God's training, I might one day come to a place of such deep trust in him that I could be brave and courageous. The Holy Spirit revealed to me that everything that I need has already been given. The "training" that I receive from God is simply how to actualize who I already am and what I've already been given.

How about you? Are you tired and worn out from struggling against your own emotions? Are you ready to see in the mirror the person who God created you to be?

Easy does it. Sit back in the saddle. Exhale deeply and pull back gently on the reins. Slow down, friend. We're almost home.

Chapter 22

The Grass is Always Greener on the Other Side of the Fence

For you 'were like sheep going astray', but now you have returned to the Shepherd and Overseer of your souls. —1 Peter 2:25

I was leaving our driveway to go to work recently one morning, and as I looked across the pasture, I thought I saw the silhouette of a horse very close to the fence line. Peering through the morning haze, I thought to myself, "Is that Hope? Is she out?" I began slowly backing up the truck, trying to get a better look. "By golly, it looks like she's out. I guess I have to go all the way back home to check for sure."

As I pulled into the yard, I noticed that she hadn't moved. "That's odd." I thought to myself. I parked the truck and began walking towards the pasture. "Yup, she's out alright. She hasn't moved from that spot, though. Son of a gun! I hope she ain't tangled in the fence!" I hurriedly went to the garage to get her halter and lead rope. Walking out to Hope, and seeing that she still hadn't moved, I felt sick in my stomach, wondering what I was going to discover. The other horses were running around whinnying at me as if they were tattling on Hope, alerting me to her plight. As I approached her, I saw that she had herself in quite the predicament. I don't know how she managed to do it, but she had gotten her entire body out of the pasture, but her left rear leg was sandwiched crisscrossed between the top and bottom wires and the middle wire. This was not the first time that she's done this. Fortunately, she has enough sense to stand and wait calmly for me.

"Easy, baby," I spoke softly to her as I put her halter on. "Ok, ya gotta just stay calm and let me help ya out of this mess." Slowly stepping on the middle wire, I pushed the wire down her leg to the ground. Stepping on the bottom wire to keep it down, I told Hope, "Foot", tugging on the hairs near her pastern, indicating that I wanted her to lift her foot. This is how I trained each of them to lift their feet so that I can clean their hooves. She carefully and calmly lifted her leg until I was able to move it between the wires and onto the other side of the fence. Then I attached the lead rope to her halter and led her back to the pasture.

On my way to work, I pondered the whole situation. Hope often gets herself into trouble because of her appetite. For her, the grass truly is always greener on the other side of the fence. She has this uncanny way of knowing when I forget to plug the electric fence in. Then she'll stick her head through and stretch as far as she can, eating to her heart's content. When she's discovered that she's stretched the wires loose enough, then she starts the process of sneaking through the fence. Most of her attempts end up successful and she's gorging herself on the grass in the field next to our property. On a few occasions, she's gotten herself stuck like she did this particular morning.

It made me think of myself and the many times that I've gotten myself into trouble sneaking out of the fence, trying to get what I thought was greener grass. As Peter said, "We all, like sheep, have gone astray." We see something that is quite appealing, and we believe that having that is better than what we already have. So, we begin testing the fence -stretching the boundaries-. We try doing everything we can to get what we want. Sometimes it works! We get what we want! Sometimes that works out ok, but other times it can cause us digestive issues (real and metaphorical). Other times, we get caught or stuck, and then we have two choices, we can either panic and try to get ourselves out of trouble, or we can sit still, humbly acknowledge our sin and wait for Jesus to rescue us. If we heed his voice and follow his instructions, he will help us out of our mess and bring us back into his pasture.

I read something a long time ago that stuck with me. It stated, "Instead of focusing on how much greener the grass is on the other side of the fence, start by watering your grass." That stuck with me, because it makes sense. Perhaps we already have everything that we need and desire, it just doesn't look like it because we've neglected it. Perhaps with time and attention, it will be transformed into what we desire. Or perhaps, we're looking at things from the wrong perspective. Perhaps if we look at what we do have with gratitude, we will see things in a way that doesn't cause us to stretch the fence to get what's on the other side. However, isn't it comforting to consider that Jesus comes to our aid every single time we get stuck, just like I do for Hope?

Now the tax collectors and sinners were all gathering around to hear Jesus. But the Pharisees and the teachers of the law muttered, 'This man welcomes sinners and eats with them.' Then Jesus told them this parable: 'Suppose one of you has a hundred sheep and loses one of them. Doesn't he leave the ninety nine in the open country and go after the lost sheep until he finds it? And when he finds it, he joyfully puts it on his shoulders and goes home. Then he calls his friends and neighbors together and says, 'Rejoice with me; I have found my lost sheep.' I tell you that in the same way there will be more rejoicing in heaven over one sinner who repents than over ninety-nine righteous persons who do not need to repent.
—Luke 15:1-7

That is the heart of our Savior. He is always out looking for the lost, and when one comes home, he welcomes him or her with rejoicing! Not shame, not condemnation, not criticism; but with joy!

Seeing the mess that we have gotten ourselves into, perhaps we're scared, perhaps we're injured or sick from our wandering; he doesn't angrily drag us back to the pasture, instead he picks us up, puts us on his shoulders and carries us home! Then he throws a celebration! That is how much he loves each one of us! Jesus goes into further detail in John 10 about his role as Shepherd and his love for his sheep. I pray that through these Scriptures that you will come to know and understand how deep Jesus' love is for you.

For the Lamb, at the center of the throne, will be their shepherd, he will lead them to springs of living water', And God will wipe every tear from their eyes. —Revelation 7:17

Chapter 23

No More Tears

He will wipe every tear from their eyes. There will be no more death, or mourning or crying or pain, for the old order of things has passed away. —**Revelation 21:4**

I don't know about you, but I've had my share of mourning, crying, and pain. I'm looking forward to the day when I'm with Jesus and all of those things will be put away with. Spring of 2019 was the beginning of a hard year for us. One day, while checking out the horses, I realized Blaze seemed lethargic. He was having difficulty walking and was barely moving. I took him to a friend's vet, who lived only a few miles from us. I explained everything to her and she did a complete physical exam on him with blood work checking for EPM and tick-borne diseases.

During the physical exam, she checked his eyes and noted that he was losing his eyesight rapidly. In fact, one eye was almost completely blind. She did X-rays on his feet and discovered some malformation on one of his toes, so she recommended that our farrier put shoes on him. His blood work came back negative for everything, so we remained baffled by his change in behavior. Blaze used to be, well, honestly, the best word to describe his old attitude is "donkey". That's right. He used to be an ass. He was dominant in the herd and bossy. He would chase the other horses for what seemed to be just the sheer joy of chasing them. It's like he enjoyed being the dominant one and took numerous opportunities to remind the herd that he was a top horse. He was obedient to us, but it was clear that he was only obedient if he felt that we respected him. This whole ordeal -whatever it was- changed him: it seemed to slow him down and took the snort out of him. To be honest, had it been under different circumstances, I wouldn't have been upset about the change, but our farrier and I both agreed that we were sad because we knew that the change was an adverse effect from something.

The shoes helped tremendously, and by the time we were able to ride him again, it was late fall. It was frustrating for me because it meant that for nearly the whole year, he was unable to be ridden, but I understood that this was for his best. He needed rest. We don't know what the coming years will hold for Blaze and us. The diagnosis of his growing blindness was a really hard thing to accept.

Tony and I discussed it, and we've agreed that no matter what, Blaze will finish his days here with us. It may be that very soon, he won't be rideable. That's okay. He's given us so many wonderful experiences and adventures that although he is still so young (at only 14 years old), we are more than glad to give him the best retirement that we can. We will do everything that we can to ensure his safety in the pasture as he continues to lose his sight.

How comforting it is to know that God offers us the same promises of comfort and security! As we come to him and remain under his guidance and care, he offers the assurance of his never-failing love and protection.

> *You are my hiding place; you will protect me from trouble and surround me with songs of deliverance.* —Psalm 32:7

> *Do not withhold your mercy from me, Lord; may your love and faithfulness always protect me.* —Psalm 40:11

> *"Because he loves me," says the Lord, I will rescue him; I will protect him, for he acknowledges my name.* —Psalm 91:14

Jesus himself prays to God for his protection for us in John 17:11-15. Paul writes in 2 Thessalonians 3:3, "But the Lord is faithful; he will strengthen you and protect you from the evil one."

One of the hardest experiences with my horses was when we had to decide to put to rest a gelding named, "Boy". We purchased him just before moving from Bemidji and only had him a few months. He was so beautiful! He looked exactly like my Brandy.

Tony was deployed to Iraq from March 2009 to March 2010. The kids and I were still living on campus at the Christian College as I was still in school. After Tony returned from Iraq, we began looking for a home near Brainerd because he was working full time out of the Brainerd National Guard Armory. We found what I had described as my dream home with 16 acres, which happened to be near Tony's childhood home. The previous owners of the home that we purchased had a carport as a shelter for livestock.

One evening my oldest son, Tim, and I were out feeding the horses. Tim noticed that Boy was standing inside the carport shelter, so he went to throw him some hay. Tim was about 14 years old at the time. He hollered at me that I should probably go to the house and get dad. I asked him why. He said to me, "Mom, Boy's bleeding pretty bad. I don't think you should come over here. Just go get dad." Tim knew my anxiety issues and how I got in emergencies. I ran to the house and told Tony, and he went outside to assess the situation. He came in the house and told me that Boy must've been kicking at flies and he kicked his rear leg through the metal siding of the carport. His hoof was nearly cut off and he's lost a lot of blood. He called our vet who came out as soon as possible. They stitched his foot back on by truck headlamp and a flashlight. Unfortunately, Boy never got better. Even though his foot healed beautifully, he couldn't walk. The vet told me that he may have gotten an infection in his joint, and if that was the case, there wasn't anything that we could do for him.

Every day he was lying down more frequently, and it was getting harder and harder for him to get up. He was also losing weight rapidly and no matter how much I tried feeding him, he just wasn't gaining any weight. Finally, I saw the writing on the wall. If he laid down in the wintertime and couldn't get up, he'd freeze to death. I knew what needed to be done. I'll never forget that day. He was lying out in the pasture, and I was having a heck of a time getting him to stand up. Finally, I said to him, "Come on buddy. You only gotta do this one more time." We called the vet and he agreed to transport him to his clinic and euthanize him. I took a piece of his mane, before loading him into the vet's trailer. I have no regrets about that decision. I knew it was the right thing to do and I'm thankful that he got to have peace.

Another horse that I've shed a lot of tears over was a huge 18h Belgian gelding. To measure a horse, you measure in "hands", with the idea being that the width of an average hand is approximately 4 inches. So, you measure from the sole of the horse's hoof to his withers, which is the raised area just at the base of his neck and meeting his back. Praus was approximately 72 inches from the ground to his withers.

I'd always loved draft horses, so when we saw this Belgian giant at the auction, I was smitten at first sight. More amazing than his size was that he was broke to ride. Needless to say, we bought him and then had to figure out how to transport him home! His name was Zeus, but I didn't like that name. I researched words, and found the Greek word, "Praus", which means "Power under control". So that became his new name. He and I bonded immediately. He had a personality similar to Goldie's in the sense that he was very loving and gentle and he gave the best hugs! I could ride him around our yard bareback and with just a halter and lead rope.

In 2015 we decided to sell our property to find something with more acreage. A few days later a strange thing happened. A man drove by our property, and seeing Praus, he stopped in and asked if he could buy him. He said that he ran a youth program and he had been looking for a Belgian. We took this as a sign from God and so we agreed to sell him. We borrowed a friend's stock trailer and hauled him to the man's house. I was in awe at how beautiful and vast the man's property was. I knew Praus would be happy there, but it didn't make my goodbye any less tearful.

I'm dreading the day when I have to say goodbye to my sweet Goldie. She's been a part of my life for 15 years now. She has been such an integral part of my growth in every aspect. I can't imagine my life without her, but I keep telling myself that she was only given to me on loan from God. As Job said, "The Lord gives and takes away." I'm thankful for the years that he's given me. I'm thankful for the lessons that he's taught me through her. I'm thankful for the adventures and joys that she and I have shared and Lord willing, we'll have more before we're through.

Whoa, there. Let's stop here and chat a bit.

Friend, let me be frank with you. If you want the assurance of being with Jesus for eternity, where there's no more sorrow, no more mourning, no more pain, no more tears, and the chance to be eternally united with loved ones, well, there's only one way. You have to accept Jesus as your Savior. Jesus, himself, says in John 14:6, "I am the way, the truth, and the life. No one comes to the Father, except through me." Acts 4:12 says, "Salvation is found in no one else, for there is no other name under heaven given to mankind, by which we must be saved."

If you declare with your mouth, Jesus is Lord, and believe in your heart that God raised him from the dead, you will be saved. —Romans 10:9

It is that simple. You don't have to do anything to earn it. In fact, you can't do anything to earn it.

For it is by grace you have been saved, through faith -and this is not from yourselves, it is the gift of God- not by works, so that no one can boast. —Ephesians 2:8-9

You see, every one of us is a sinner. Even if we can avoid sinning outwardly, we still sin in our hearts. Jesus said that if we hate someone in our heart, that's equivalent to murder (Matthew 5:21-23). He also said that if anyone lusts after another person, that's equivalent to committing adultery. What he's saying is that the standard for holiness is so high that there's no way that any one of us can do it in our strength.

Isaiah 64:6 states, "All of us have become like one who is unclean, and all of our righteous acts are like filthy rags." What Isaiah is getting at here, is that even if we were able to keep all of the commands perfectly, all of our "perfection" is still filthy because deep down inside, we'd more than likely have the sin of pride in our hearts. We are so good at looking at ourselves through rose-colored glasses, excusing and justifying our behavior, that we are blind to the deceitfulness in our hearts. We can even convince ourselves that whatever we're doing is for the good of someone else or God, without realizing that deep down inside, we want to use our good works to glorify ourselves.

There's only one way that we can have friendship with God, and that's through accepting Jesus' sacrifice for our sins and applying his payment to our debt. God has provided this pardon to us as a gift. All we need to do is simply accept it.

Isaiah 55:6 says, "Seek the Lord while he may be found; call on him while he is near." Time is of the essence, my friend. You have nothing to lose and everything to gain. As we untack and put the horses away, let me pray for ya.

Father in heaven, thank you for the person reading these pages. I pray, Father, that you would meet him/her right where they are at. I pray that you would provide whatever their heart needs. I pray that if he/she hasn't given their lives to you that you would help them in their hesitation. I pray that you would help them open their heart to you and receive your forgiveness and that they would enter into the fellowship of believers. Bring Godly people to them to teach and encourage them on this new journey. For the person reading this who has given his or her life to you, please guide and direct them in discovering their gifts and talents that you have given them. Please help them to develop those gifts and talents to use to bless those around them and glorify you, God. I pray that you would place a burden upon their hearts for those who are poor in spirit and broken. Father, open doors of opportunity for them to bless others, and be blessed in the doing so. Thank you, Jesus, for everything that you have done and everything that you will continue to do in their lives. Amen.

God bless ya, friend! I look forward to seeing you out on the trail again!

Glossary

Bit, A metal piece that is attached to a bridle and inserted into a horse's mouth.

Blaze, *Intransitive verb*: to be conspicuously brilliant or resplendent. *Verb:* to lead in some direction or activity (Merriam-Webster Dictionary)

Bridle, A piece of equipment used to direct a horse. It includes both the headstall that holds a bit that goes in the mouth of a horse, and the reins that are attached to the bit.

Halter, a strap or rope placed around the head of a horse or other animal, used for leading or tethering it.

Rein, A long, narrow strap attached at one end to a horse's bit, typically used in pairs to guide or check a horse in riding or driving.

Tack, *Noun*: equipment or accessories equipped on horses and other equines in the course of their use as domesticated animals. *Verb*: fasten or fix in place with tacks.

ABOUT
KHARIS PUBLISHING

KHARIS PUBLISHING is an independent, traditional publishing house with a core mission to publish impactful books, and channel proceeds into establishing mini-libraries or resource centers for orphanages in developing countries, so these kids will learn to read, dream, and grow. Every time you purchase a book from Kharis Publishing or partner as an author, you are helping give these kids an amazing opportunity to read, dream, and grow. Kharis Publishing is an imprint of Kharis Media LLC. Learn more at

https://www.kharispublishing.com.